HUMAN BODIES
NEW AND COLLECTED POEMS 1987-1999

HUMAN BODIES

NEW AND COLLECTED POEMS 1987-1999

BY

MARILYN BOWERING

WITH AN INTRODUCTION BY DAVE GODFREY

Porcepic Books
an imprint of
Beach Holme Publishing, Vancouver

Copyright © 1999 by Marilyn Bowering

First Edition

All rights reserved.

No part of this book may be reproduced or transmitted in any form by any means, electronic or mechanical, including photocopying, recording or any information storage, retrieval and transmission systems now known or to be invented, without permission in writing from the publisher, except by a reviewer who may quote brief passages in a review.

This book is published by Beach Holme Publishing, #226—2040 West 12th Ave., Vancouver, BC, V6J 2G2. This is a Porcepic Book.

We acknowledge the generous assistance of The Canada Council and the BC Ministry of Small Business, Tourism and Culture.

Editor: Dave Godfrey
Production and Design: Teresa Bubela
Cover Art by Mercedes Carbonell
Printed in Canada.

Canadian Cataloguing in Publication Data

Bowering, Marilyn, 1949-
  Human bodies

Poems.
"A Porcépic Book".
ISBN 0-88878-395-7

I. Title.
PS8553.O9H85 1999   C811'.54   C99-910308-3
PR9199.3.B635H85 1999

*For Michael and Xan
and for my mother*

Table of Contents

✧ ✧ ✧

An Introduction by Dave Godfrey   i

Anyone Can See I Love You
    Norma Jean   4
    Husband One: Jim   5
    Summer 1946   6
    Job Offers   7
    Miss Golden Dreams Calendar   8
    Driving to Red Rock Dairy   9
    The Yankee Clipper, Joe Dimaggio   10
    Last night after we were in bed   11
    Fairy Tale Marriage, January 14, 1954   12
    Precious Little Girl   13
    Korea Winter 1954   14
    San Francisco   15
    Pink Elephants   15
    The Divorce, October 1954   16
    Minor Surgery, Fall 1954 - Winter 1955   17
    New Year, New York, January 1, 1955   18
    Interview, Summer 1956   19
    If someone doesn't mention my name   20
    Desire   21
    On the Farm in Connecticut, 1956-57   22
    The gods punish those   23
    Second Baby, November 1958   24
    Let's Make Love - Yves Montand, Spring 1960   25
    Let's Make Love II   26
    The Misfits, Reno, Nevada   27
    Westside Hospital, L.A., August 1960   28
    Method Acting   28
    I have this dream in which men in white jackets   29
    Finocchio's, San Francisco October 1960   30
    Dr. Kris: Interpreting Dreams   30
    After Arthur, Payne-Whitney Clinic, Winter 1961   31

Table of Contents Continued...

In My Own Words	33
For Clark Gable	33
The Dress	34
Best Wishes	35
After Arthur Left	35
Happy Birthday, Mr. President, May 1962	36
Red Stockings	37
This is My House, Spring 1962	38
Whether the door to the house is black or not	42
The Dressing Room, August 4-5, 1962	42
Three husbands, not too many, just enough	44
I dreamed that my nipples	44
They came to look	45
A walled garden, a small chapel	45

Grandfather was a Soldier   47

Calling All the World   85

Love As It Is
Antiquities

I Have Been Dreaming About the Wife	113
Being True	114
The Red Factory	114
Christmas in Prague, 1986	115
Native Land	116
My Dear Friends	117
Madrigal, a Lullaby for Xan	119
Letter from Portugal	119
Tranquille	120
Flowers	122
Antiquities	123

The Mercers

The House at Mercer's Cove	124
In the Front Room	125
When the Men are Gone to Sea	126

TABLE OF CONTENTS CONTINUED...

I Lie Down	127
I Touched the Swelling	128
The Black Horse	128
One Heater to Heat the Whole House	129
Eight Poems for Margaret, July-August, 1989	
The packers are done	129
She dreams of falling	130
A white butterfly	131
The moon rose upside down	132
My bed is my island	133
I sit up in bed	134
The wind shakes the trees	134
Now is the time	136
A Cold Departure: The Liaison of George Sand and Fryderyk Chopin	
George Sand's Letter	137
Chopin's Letters	159

AUTOBIOGRAPHY
The Mind's Road to Love
The Mind's Road to Love	171
In the evening I found you.	171
A Reflection on Ecstasy and its Limitation	173
Natural Powers	178
Gifts of Grace	181
About Your Name	183

Nature's Children
Nature's Children	185

Autobiography
Autobiography	187
I was born	187
I know that by these few remarks	191
The appearances began	191
I would have wept	193
I remember	194
Awakening in time	194

TABLE OF CONTENTS CONTINUED...

How Were The People Made?
On the Making of People — 195
How Were the People Made? — 200
Mirror Gazing — 208
Interior Castle
Interior Castle — 219
She Goes Away — 223

WHEN I AM DEAD AND MY HEART IS WEIGHED
Emblems
Dog — 229
Apple — 230
Father — 231
Mercury — 232
Self — 232
Star — 233
Mirror — 233
Time — 234
Eleven Short Poems for Mercedes to Draw — 234
Notes From the Dead — 238
Letter to Janey — 241
Gruta de las Maravillas — 262

Acknowledgements and Notes — 269

The Art of Intelligent Indeterminacy

In periods of social certainty, and arrogance, the work of the poet often plays the role of an escape valve, a breathing hole cut into the great floes of conformity and sameness which threaten those who have not given in to the common beliefs. Such artists, Rimbaud or Coleridge, are content, for a time, to gravitate to the boundaries of civilization. But in a period such as ours, where only a few certainties are fashionable and indeterminancy has its own critical language and priesthood, the work of the poet, however excellent, is likely to disappear in the fogs of social rant and media banality.

In such a world, Marilyn Bowering's poems provide a mapping towards a hard-won and individual cohesion. Their initial pleasure, the bouquet, is in precision of language and deftness of narrative, but this poetry ages well, not least because of the intelligent mind that lies behind it and the ongoing search for compassion and understanding which informs the whole body of work.

> The man stands on a platform.
> We are born so that we may die, he says.
> And I see—
> the me that holds an apple and eats it, making a wheel round the middle, then eating the 'spokes' at each end—
> this me is already dead.
> After a while he kneels on the red platform carpet showing the soles of his shoes.
>
> I lie awake at night. I am here and I am dead,
> just like you Janey when I last saw you.

We know almost immediately where we are and whose story we are momentarily a part of. Although Bowering is always willing to explore uncertainties or the fragilities of our senses and intelligence, she never leaves us without at least one set of slash marks to guide us through the mists and forests.

Chief among these is the importance of character. Bowering's poems almost always put us face to face with people: whether it is Marilyn Monroe or Monsieur and Madame Schuyère, Fryderyk Chopin or the mysterious Alexei Folchakov, the strange Mr. Cook, maker of people, or the finely sketched and uncatchable Janey, the "child who remembers a ribbon of time." These poems are not simply meditations or commentaries; many of them take their fundamental shape from specific lives, and their dreams, desires and fears, all rich in both nuance and variation.

And these characters move through real worlds, resonant with specificity. Bowering never denies the unavoidability of social impact. Like a poetic, one-woman NFB, but without the political bias, she gives full rein to the forces of the world that shape, and distort, character. At times, this is tongue-in-cheek: "The eye is a prism. Mr. Folchakov has one / glass eye which he wears like a medal from the / last war." At times, ironic:

> They screamed: 'Monchan! Monchan!
> Precious Little Girl!'
>
> It was a kind of confetti
> for mourning:
>
> fires lit on an altar,
> smoke bubbling to Fuji,
> a sweet, sweet scent
> of bombs and mutilation.
> It was the right country to come to
> after the wedding.

At times, it sets emotion against concept:

> Here is my body, Lord.
> It melts like wax. It is a candle in the earth.

He said, Give, give, give.

*I shall represent for him an Italy
which one visits and enjoys on spring days
but where one cannot remain permanently,
because there is more sunshine than beds and tables.*

At times, it shows the wisdom of innocence:

When you are jist a baby they take you.
They wrap you up in a shawl that belonged to yr granny
and they take you to the church. It is such a big church,
with a balcony and a pipe organ
and pillars lik the ones they tied Samson to.
If you sits at a wall end you canna see round the pillars.

So I likes to sit next to the aisle, and I cn turn round and see the
mommies and daddys when they stand at the back until the preacher
notices them and he calls out:
Who brings this child?
And they answer, We do, and he says,
Bring the child forth. And the wee baby is carried up by the Mum,
but it is the Dad who hands it over when they're at the front
and the Preacher says, Do you dedicate this baby to Jesus?
The Dad hands you over and the preacher takes you in his big paws,
with the congregation lookin on, and that's that.

And at times it merely documents the realities of the tribal community,
both its horrors:

Two soldiers carry the white wrapped lower half
of a man.
They have strapped him onto a bar
(as water carriers would) between them.
They have made him a seat and toe rest,

although there is nothing to him above waist level.

> Inside are the "fosses",
> holes dug under roots into the chalk soil
> where 26 years later twenty-seven bodies—
> members of the Résistance—will lie
>
> > (from "Grandfather was a Soldier")

and its small joys.

> As when the the 1st battalion
> of the West African Frontier Regiment
>
> played, for her, the Hausa Farewell
> as she left Nigeria,
>
> so now there is a salute to be given.
>
> Let the wind give it,
> and the trees.
>
> > (from "Eight Poems for Margaret")

Nonetheless, one would never describe these works as value free. Like Yeats, Bowering accepts the poet's need to confront the requirements and imperatives of belief, personal belief as well as community. Her friend Robin Skelton found a magic in books and read profusely; she does also. For scholars, there is probably a life time of work in tracking all the influences and allusions, but perceptive readers, comparing one poem to another and noting similarities and icons, will find on their own the counter-weights to her diversities, inklings of that driving set of probabilities which inspire and inform her works, both poetic and fictional. This is a deeper reward of reading Bowering, for this set of probabilities is not a carefully defended potager, with the wilderness fitted into rows and squares and triangles, hedged with box, but a trellis work, a scaffolding, capable of expansion and perspective, capable of adding in the unique and the unusual, the mundane and the iconic.

As you read the poems, and compare one to another, you cannot but become aware of the very North American sense of reflective worlds; not a simple division into fact and theory, reality and symbol, artifact and spirit, but a balancing and comparison of worlds, each whole and complete in its own, but each providing reflections on and illuminations of any other and all together. There are values here, some worth a penny and some worth a pound, but they are not the values of the Preacher, but of the Mum, or of the child herself.

> The past and future
> Have proven their argument
> Against ours.

Human Bodies comprises six sections. These are collected poems and only small changes have been made to the first five books. The last section contains poems new to this book. Together, they make a cellar of vintage wine. One not to be drunken down in a single riotous night, but to be selected carefully and savoured, depending on time, mood and circumstances.

Anyone Can See I Love You was published in 1987. It remains a model for the poetic rendering of the public person, setting the small mundanities of that very public life against an almost mythic vitalization of the inner life of Norma Jean.

> and I want to tell you
> there's a black halo around the world
>
> and a dark angel who is my lover.
> I can't eat,
> I can't sleep,
> but I'm sure to recover.

Also published in 1987, *Grandfather was a Soldier* is more than it appears and requires some work on the reader's part. On the surface, it deals with one Canadian soldier out of the 619,636 who joined up as part of Canada's support of the great imperial misadventure of the century. Deeper down lies a meditation on death and memory. What is it that we remember; how do we remember?

But this is the Somme and there are 1777 unidentified dead
in one field's small cemetery...plus
Adanac, Regina Trench, Mouquet Farm.

Imagine the first ploughing—metal, wire, stone—
and the first growth...
a snail crawls over the back of a gravestone.

Grandson, ghost and guide come together as we move through the cemetery and battlefield. And move apart. A page of the visitor's book is examined, removed, burned. There is an enormity to this past which defeats synthesis. Perhaps the mythic will help provide some cohesion:

Each night
the river opens her belly and out come
ducks, a white swan, myriads of fish,
and a man, dressed in black, with his boat.
He offers eventual meeting
with the boundary walkers.

Perhaps not, perhaps there is only the attempt to define or remake one single person:

Even when the sunflowers and sun join
And the horse's whinny becomes the breath of the beast
outside the flimsy safety of the tent; even when
we know what we believe, the past and future have
proven their argument
against ours.

Experience cannot keep its single thread,
and a thousand dreams fail—
as does invaluable love—

but I know your face.

Calling All the World is an intelligent jest, an antidote to too much news of the everyday, a delicacy that Leacock and Pratt might have combined on if they had been present at this moment in time, "...as Mr. Folchakov takes out a telescope to / view Alexander the Great running alongside a / train as it nears a border."

Even here, however, the search for comprehension and compassion continues. Laika, the moongrel, the mutnik, the pupnik, the woofnik, struggles to make sense out of this experience and to calm her own fears and terror. Mr. Folchakov struggles also, against time and within memory and imagination. And accepts help from wherever it comes. It is, indeed, Prokofiev who helps them, as well as the woman in blue, as both man and dog move "way beyond your imagining":

> We journey west.
> We follow sun and moon.
> Ocean leads to land to ocean.
> There is just one circle,
> this earth we know.

Love As It Is consists of a series of individual poems plus "A Cold Departure", an imaginative reconstruction of the love/relationship of George Sand and Fryderyk Chopin. Male and female, dark ships with only the smallest of rigging lights passing at close quarters in a dark night, invisible except for the damage they cause.

> *One need not fully record all that has been said and done. Mme Sand can have nothing but good memories of me in her heart, if she ever looks back on the past...it is a fever for which there is no cure in cases where the imagination is so dominant and the victim is let loose on shifting and uncertain ground. Well, they say "even a cypress-tree may have its caprices."*

Almost as though this was a challenge to her, Bowering records with great fidelity the "other" than good memories which Mme Sand certainly did have:

> All winter I have watched the light fade,
>
> all spring I have waited for your hand
> to lift me above the round world
> like the moon
>
> like the womb that dreamed me,
>
> like the spin
> of a foreign sea.

Although very personal and precise, this poem functions much like a play and benefits from Bowering's involvement with both CBC and BBC in the production of radio/poetic/drama.

Autobiography, 1996, contains the poem I reread most often: "The Mind's Road to Love", which, to me, is Blakean in its mirrored simplicity and complexity. Here, Bowering makes clear her long term determination to begin "to think of the actual / existence of things."

Few modern poets could, or would dare to, bring such metaphysical challenges and complexity into their work; only one or two could make it work. Even the titles are indicative of her willingness to take chances.

2.
A Reflection on Ecstasy and its Limitations

> In the mirror of the actual existence of things
> is God,
>
> in so far as He or She has tracked through DNA.
> Therefore, in consideration of this, in all creatures
>
> such as you, that enter my mind through my hands and
> lips
>
> through the open nerve ends of the framework of light
> in which I walk,

through the electrical nature of the universe,
in you all creatures have entered my heart.

Many of the individual poems in both *Autobiography* and *When I am Dead and My Heart is Weighed* draw, it appears to me, from the challenging explorations presented in "The Mind's Road to Love", as though Bowering has been able to move on to an easier and more graceful representation of life once this major map room of the emblematic has been completed. "How were the People Made?" shares much of the light-hearted irony of Laika and Mr. Folchakov, but it also has the range and wit of Lessing's *Shikasta* and a playful reworking of some of the themes and tropes of "west coast" poetry and of Bowering's own habitual symbols: *How were the People Made?*

They were made with a blanket of stars,
they were drawn across the universe

until they were in shreds.
they were made to open their eyes

in moonlight, they were forced to watch
starshells and artillery bursts,

they were ordered to re-define light.
They were wired up to EEGs,

they were cross-referenced with earthquakes

The longer poem, "Letter to Janey", is also a work which can be read in counterpoint to "The Mind's Road to Love". There is a narrator and there is Janey, a double, an alter ego, but a being as real, if not more real, than the narrator herself.

Then I do go, Janey, I have to,
and I come to a hole in the ground—
a collapsed tunnel.
Around the rim is dry broken earth,
dead grass, pale sliced rock;

> Go and help her, they say,
> She's hurt.

Life for Bowering is never certain, but never totally terrifying. Imperfect tools though they are, mind and heart must be put to use and are. Realities "slip through the mesh of memory / like a small silver fish" but even as they pass, the poet makes the attempt to turn them into that "ribbon of time" which give us the strength to go down into the quarry yet again, when necessary.

Bowering's is a voice which now goes from strength to strength. Her range continues to grow and the lines appear truer and easier with each work. Like the good Italian wines of Alba, Brusnengo or Carema, the poems improve with age and with comparison. They need to breathe, in your mind. They need to be savoured. Her terrain can be difficult and her references are definitely not all available in her footnotes, but for those who learn to appreciate her many qualities, I suspect these pages will be well-worn and I trust and hope that few books from this printing will last more than a year or so without being "ruined" by notes, reflections and interrogatories. Investors in the crowd are advised to buy a second copy for the vault.

Dave Godfrey

...the poet cannot proceed in this way, and must depend in life on that zone of shadow and fog that floats around human bodies.

— *Luis Cernuda*

Anyone Can See I Love You

Did I tell you the most beautiful thing I ever saw? It was a stone, down by the pier in Santa Monica where my mother used to go to find her dates. The sun was just going down, the whole sky was pink— like a birthday cake. I was walking on the beach in bare feet and I stubbed my toe on this rock. It hurt like hell so I hopped around for a minute and swore and picked the rock up. I was just going to throw it. Instead, I don't know why, I held it up to the light. It was grey until then, but held up to the light it glowed like something alive. Small and warm in my hand. It was like everything in the world *was* that way, and all you had to do was pick it up, touch it.

Norma Jean

Jim was my first husband. Jim Dougherty.
I don't know why I married him except
I was sixteen,
I was Norma Jean, an orphan:
that is, my mother was mad,
I had no father.

Jim had a job,
and a car that slid along the highway
like oil over glass.

We had a dog, a house.
I kept the house clean,
I walked the dog
oh long walks all the way to the pier
where the sailors were.

Jim didn't like me to spend
so much money on clothes.
He wanted us to save
like other couples.

But how could I stop knowing what I knew?
I had no home. I had no one.
He couldn't change that,
though I skinned rabbits,
I cut up fish for him.

At that time I would do anything.

Well, it was his choice to go away.
It was war time,
but he did the leaving.

I went to work,
and when a man came with a camera
(stalking the assembly line like a hunter)
it was a fated encounter with a mirror.

We both came up gasping
(the camera between us).
He thought he was making money.
He thought he was making Norma Jean.

So how did I know I had to change,
sense that I was born blond
but that someone had made a mistake with the colour,
like mixing beer with champagne?

Someone had lost me at the beginning
and nobody claimed me but a city.
L.A. had to feed me,
L.A. had to
not let me die.

I lightened my hair, closed my smile a little.
They said they needed to see my mouth quiver...

alteration so minor....

It was right.
It was hopeless.

You change skins,
you wriggle in to 'Marilyn',
it's the real you inside looking out,

but Norma Jean is somewhere asking—
did anybody love her?—

Never.

Husband One: Jim

I knew that I loved you.
I was dying. The car slewed off the road
as the deer stepped out in front
in the mountains where Jim and I went hunting.

Had it seen us together?
Had we taken its mate?
I don't know,

but it waited until I drove that way alone.

It was hooded in snow,
its mouth red as a kiss in the headlights.

When I died—I remember to the depths of my heart—
I said that I loved you.
It was in my mind
like the taste of peach or plum.

When I died the car flew apart
like a jelly-glass.
In my heart was a message: 'I love you',
as if it could stop me from being punished.

I don't know.
The way I hurt things.
You have to choose sometimes....

It was clear as a map,
it was unforgiveable,
your voice louder than the crash
(I was part of the roadway,
a black wet smear)
saying: I love you / I love you /
I love you.

Summer 1946

Jim was in Shanghai, on his ship,
when he got my letter.

You see I couldn't be married
and sign a movie contract.
They thought I might get pregnant
and quit.

There were so many blanks.
I had to have training
as a starlet.
What would I say if asked who I was?
Married to Jim?
My mother, mad, in an L.A. asylum?

I became more negotiable
after the divorce.

There were a lot of calls for blonds.
People knew what they wanted....

I kept Jim's car.
He phoned me once and asked,
'Are you happy?'

I said I was lonely at night.

This made him angry,
and he disappeared,
forever,
out of my life.

Job Offers

First they say
you've got it,
you're the best,

then somebody thinks you're
too blond
or dumb,

or you want too much money,

then it's on again,

but you don't hear

and don't hear,

then some stranger calls up and says
Baby you'd better come through,

then nobody calls

and you do a few more covers,

and you wave at an important man
in a big car,

and he says

*Honey I can't talk now
but I've got a job for you
come and see me about it
later
at my house.*

Miss Golden Dreams Calendar

I lie down on red velvet—
my body is an alabaster arc,
my head is thrown back—blond
hair like a vortex,
red lips and nipples,
perfect thighs tapering
to perfect toes.

It was how I imagined
I would look. I could feel
men want to touch
through the lens:

what they wouldn't unlock
for me!

All the hands
that couldn't touch.

I lay back satisfied.
For the first time in months
I slept.

Artists said it was perfect symmetry.

I lay down naked on red velvet,
and for a moment the world I wanted
began,

and the other one stopped.

Driving to Red Dock Dairy

I drove all the way to the desert,
then I made a phone call.
To the east—
an ocean of sand,
date palm country,

my father.

Hello. Is Mr. Gifford there?

Who's calling him? (a woman's voice)

This is Marilyn. I'm his child... I mean,
the little girl years ago. Gladys Baker's daughter.

*I don't know who you are
But I'll tell him you're on the phone.*

(a minute or two of silence)

*He doesn't want to see you.
He suggests you see his lawyer in Los Angeles
if you have some complaint. Do you have a pencil?*

No, I don't have a pencil.
Goodbye.

The Yankee Clipper, Joe Dimaggio

One blind date,

and then we went fishing,

Surf foamed on the beach,
the foam blew in drifts,

I cast,
and reeled in,
and threw back.

We were immortal:

no shadows,
just sun and salt,
and then the dark.

As we drove down the freeway,
I saw a grey wisp
spiralling far behind.

It was my mother,
It was all the past.

Wind and salt
and the fast road
into night.

Joe dressed like a banker,
Kept his life balanced;
I came in
on his blind side.

But he kept his word,
he loved me.

He could hold,
he could laugh.

White cuffs brushing
gold dark wrists:

he made the prison I wanted
with his body.

He took me home.
I had fish scent on my hands,
my lips were rimed with salt.

I had taken the bait,
I had risen to his silence.

Last night after we were in bed,

no, after we were asleep,
after the light was out,
and I rolled over you and you said
you wanted to sleep on the other side
and then we rolled back,

well, I lay my head on your arm,
and then we both turned once
and I turned back
and then I was alone.

Let me tell you:
it was just me
and this wild animal—
it came into the basement
through a split in the wall.
it climbed the stairs
into the hallway.

I ran through the house
but it kept right behind me.

Then you were there
and it stood over you
and was going to kill you,

and I threw my shoe at it
and it dropped you
and turned back to me.

I ran out of the house screaming.

Everyone had come out of their houses to watch.

I looked back,
I could see your face at the window.

Then, just like that,
the animal vanished.

I went home and shut all the doors and windows.

You know I love animals.
Why would I have a dream like that?

Fairy Tale Marriage
January 14, 1954

For luck Joe had on
the same polka-dot tie
he'd worn when we met,

and a dark suit,
a white shirt,
glossy black shoes.

The Sex Queen
and
The Slugger:

Joe was one story,
I was another.

He was the Yankee Clipper,
the Power Hitter,
my Slugger with the ideal
batting average.

And I was Cinderella,
out of tinsel,
in a high-necked brown suit
with ermine collar.

A hundred reporters waited
at City Hall in San Francisco;

and we sped away to the mountains,

snow above us,
the desert below.

Precious Little Girl

In Japan, when I arrived with Joe
not long after the wedding,
the people
(faces pale with anguish
and grief—they are a nation
of self-immolation)

stormed the plane.
They screamed: 'Monchan! Monchan!
Precious Little Girl!'

It was a kind of confetti
for mourning:

fires lit on an altar,
smoke bubbling to Fuji,
a sweet, sweet scent

of bombs and mutilation.
It was the right country to come to
after the wedding.

But Joe thought grief
was an insult.
And 'Monchan! Monchan!
Precious Little Girl!'

wasn't his idea of a wife.

Korea, Winter 1954

Snowflakes
on a plum sequinned dress,
bare shoulders, pale breasts,

snowflakes swirled over
the runway.

I leaned out of the helicopter,
waving,

Soldiers clung to the watch towers.

When I sang
they were a warm surging sea.
When I stooped, they moaned.

The war in Korea needed me.
I was the opposite,
a familiar embrace,
I was everything ever dreamed.

I was Marilyn Monroe.

And they—
recognized me.

San Francisco

In San Francisco,
where we lived,
I liked the hills
but nothing else.

It was cold.
The wind hurt my face.

At night, when Joe was home,
I stood on the back porch
looking at the lights in the distance.

Sometimes we went to his restaurant,
but people forgot to eat,
and business suffered.

I rode the cable cars,
I got lost in the fog,

and when I came home
Joe was angry.

He was moody,
sober,
dignified.

Pink Elephants

Joe is in the audience.

The circus elephant is sprayed pink.
It wears a harness on its head—
wide pink leather straps
studded with rhinestones.

I sit high up,
holding just above its ears.

I wear net stockings,
black velvet, white satin,
jewels on my ears, neck.
A spray of ostrich plumes sways
at my back.

It's for charity,
for the lost, the sick,
drunks, addicts,

everyone I will become
or leave,
or imagine I see
on the white walls of a dark room
after midnight.

(I thought I saw Joe in the audience.)

The Divorce, October 1954

He didn't talk to me.
He was cold.
He was indifferent to me as a human being
and an artist.
He didn't want me to have friends of my own.
He didn't want me to do my work.
He watched television instead of talking to me.

We just lived in two different worlds.

You see,
every man is different.

It's like having amnesia
and starting all over.

You go into a clinic,
someone takes your name,

your history,
you change clothes.

In a while you come out

and everything about you is rearranged.

Minor Surgery
Fall 1954-Winter 1955

Each time under the anesthetic
I almost forget.
After the needle bite,
the taste of garlic seeped under the tongue—

no interval.

Then a nurse asks, 'Who's your doctor?
What's his name?'

And I have, I have let it slip.
It comes back in a second, slowly
as opening a present, untieing the ribbon,
lifting the lid of the box,

the first guess is the right one,
the first guess says what's in it,

me, as always,
a confection invented for this very moment.

I am anxious about the future.
I am on my own,
my course fixed, irreversible,
taking myself apart,
fracturing the crystal,
separating its colours:

a new career
in analysis,
in love.

Real people,
real problems,
some inner meaning,
some band striking up,

secret meetings in Manhattan
and Brooklyn Heights.

Arthur Miller is back in my life.

It was like running into a tree!
You know—like a cool drink when you've got a fever.
You see my toe—this toe? Well he sat and held my toe
and we just looked into each other's eyes all
evening.

New Year, New York
January 1, 1955

The year is changing,
expanded,
gilded,

or
stunned beyond recognition—

all life on this planet
is a film gone too far;
it comes to a bad end.

it is late, past midnight,
the church is empty,
the beach opens its palm to show
a starfish orange as a lily.

18

All living things blend,

become sunrise.

I watch the flight of birds
low down on the horizon,
their pattern broken, together,
broken.

It's like in the ark
where the animals enter two by two,

only some are one-winged, one-legged,
lost,
their pinions clipped,

led

by what memories of silver sea,
of the early morning estuary?

Interview, Summer 1956

Some women want to own men.
They think men should belong to them,
should co-ordinate like a pair of shoes.

I like a man to be independent.
Look at Arthur.
No one tells him what to do,
and he stands up for his friends.

They say he's a communist.
A communist is for the people, right?

I'm for the people.
Arthur is for me.

All he has to do is love me. Perfectly.
Do you understand?

He's not jealous like Joe.
You see a lot of men want me,
but they won't give.

It's like when you're hungry or thirsty.

But I need to eat and drink too.

Love is simple.
To understand
you have to look from the inside.

What do I need?
I need someone to hold me.

When I'm afraid
and I don't believe in anything,

I need Arthur to hold me.

Only,

he can't fail.

If someone doesn't mention my name,

if they know there is something in you
not thinking of me,
that wants to be alone,
that doesn't always need me;

if someone doesn't think of me
when they think of you,

if you can walk into a room
and not come first to me:

whatever your reasons are,
they are not enough.

I know what I'm talking about,
I've been thinking about love
all my life.

It has few colours.
It is blond.
It is black.

Desire

We share this excitement, strangeness.
It comes on suddenly—a seizure.
It achieves hatred, fear.

Men think desire evolves through stages,
grub to larva to fully coloured creature.

No.
It is all one moment of strange beauty.

But Marilyn, remember on the beach where they crowded you
saying, 'Show us more, Marilyn,'
and they began to chant and touch;
they wanted a scrap of you,
they wanted flesh
in a thousand pieces, a sacrifice.

And we swam out in the water
and someone came in a boat to rescue us.

Marilyn, you almost drowned.

But you have to take desire
and use it like a knife.
You have to want to rape:

everyone is a stranger,
and there's no real giving
but by force, by hurt.

On the Farm in Connecticut, 1956-57

I've had one pregnancy so far.
The baby died.
The thing I can't forget
is that it *was* alive....

So we came to this farm.
Hugo, Arthur's dog, liked it a lot.
There was so much space.
I put in new windows so we could sit together
and watch it.

Then Arthur started working.
He built himself a cabin
about thirty yards from the house.

Am I like that?
Could I accept that?

The cat brought in dead birds;
and the bull calves were sold
as soon as they were weaned from the mother.
They're of no use.

I've had it explained over and over.

And I remembered Jim, my first husband,
stopping the car once when we were coming back
from a hunting trip.

He reached in the back
to strangle a deer that had
started to come to life.

One day Arthur crossed the grass between his study
and the house.
I was watching the cat.

Arthur cleaned his feet at the door
and then—I could tell he'd been thinking about it—

asked:

*What would you do, Marilyn,
if you met a wild animal
while you were out on your own—
remember there's no man with a gun—*

*and this creature runs on all fours towards you?
Think about it.
The animal is black,
it is hungry,
it doesn't know who you are.*

I would show it water, Arthur.
I would give it my face to hold in its paws.
I would unstitch the hair from my head, the dark
and the light.
I would put my bare head into its mouth.
I would look as far inside as I could.
Then I would scream,
then I would die, Miller.

Do you call that suicide?

That's what I thought I said.

Then I went into the hospital.
Then we moved back to New York.

The gods punish those

who open eyes underground.

Cut their wings off
pull them apart

tie them to a bed
and make them fit

lift the womb out
deliver

two white butterflies.

Second Baby, November 1958

Mr. Miller had his own bathroom,
kept his clothes in the hall closet,
he had lunch alone,
walked the dog alone.

I lived in my bedroom.

I didn't drink champagne
or take sleeping pills.

I didn't want to hurt the baby.

I stopped looking at myself
naked.
I lay in bed all day.
Lost the baby.

There were no flowers or cards....

What kind of a life is it...?

Mr. Miller didn't like to go out.
Mr. Miller seemed
a distant husband.

I ate everything I could:
lamb chops, pasta,
a dozen eggs.

I cried and cried.

Got dressed, did my hair, make-up,
took it all off, cried,
started again.

I didn't want to disappoint
Mr. Miller.

Let's Make Love—Yves Montand
Spring 1960

First I was dancing
with a stranger.
The first dance, the main one
that shapes the evening.
We were out of step
but our bodies shivered
where they touched.

He was teaching me
new steps.

Forward
back
back.

And around.

We slid along the mirror lake
to the horizon.
The glass reflected
perfect unison

back back
forward.

And around.

We were two white swans
neck to neck.

Arthur glimmered at the edge.
He was a distant star,
he was something forgotten
in the firmament.

Yves
had other interests.
First things first.
Me.

And he looked like Joe.
And he was there
teaching me
new steps
on the dance floor.

Let's Make Love II

Mr. Miller locks himself in his study.
He won't come out.
I keep telling him

(dear God this scream
is stuck in my throat),

I'm your wife, your wife!

I feel in love with Yves.
I could start again.
He is ambitious—

Piaf,
Simone Signoret,
Marilyn Monroe—

his affairs
advance.
I dance in my bedroom singing
'C'est si bon, si bon',
and do a soft shoe.

Arthur leaves me alone on purpose.

The Misfits, Reno, Nevada

You know it's bad luck
to return to the scene of a divorce.

You should throw your ring into the river,
give up;

but there are nightmares
and pain,

and a whole god-damned
tableful of Nembutal,
alcohol,
ice.

We sit up all night.
Arthur suffers and weeps,
I test my heart—yes, it breaks,
no, it doesn't remember happiness.

Arthur has written me a script called,
'The Misfits'.

The long waits,
the need to get it over;
we give the performances of our lives
in Nevada.

The real thing,
everything turned around all the way.

You see?

I am playing myself
with no centre, drifting

on set and off;

can't sleep
in this nest of vultures
desert heat.

**Westside Hospital, L.A.
August 1960**

I take pills
to get me through the night
so I won't have to see Arthur
so I won't have to think,

and I've found my way
to eternity,
though I'm not sure it's what
I expected.

It's sweet revenge, Arthur;

but now that's over
and I'm on my way
from one drug to another,

and I want to tell you
there's a black halo around the world

and a dark angel who is my lover.

I can't eat,
I can't sleep,
but I'm sure to recover.

Method Acting

With what do I make contact?

It's the nailhead,
not just the blow.

I try my scenes over
probing the nerve of
a rape,
a mad mother;

or the orphanage helps
to get the face right
to get the laugh.

Arthur discovers
sores in my mouth
(there's my mother
scratching at her wrist
with a knife):

I can't remember
The last time we kissed.

I am trying to find my art,
my sorcery,
my mirror.

I have no way out.

Take this heart
and watch it beating,
genuine.

Is it living?
Is it dead?
Is the moment between
caught on film?

I have this dream in which men in white jackets

come into the house and they put me in a strait
jacket. I keep screaming at them, 'There's nothing
wrong with me!' But they won't listen. They're
wearing white masks. I don't recognize any of
them. They put me into a white hearse and they
take me back to the orphanage. We go inside, one
iron door after another slamming behind me. I
scream and scream, hitting my head against the
iron bars until I have no more breath.

And then?

Nothing. They leave me there.

Finocchio's, San Francisco October 1960

Then this woman comes on, breathless,
sewn into a skin-tight sequinned gown.

Her hair is wind-blown, platinum.
She takes tiny steps around the floor,
wiggling her rear.

Her lips quiver.

She cups her breasts:

I love you all. You're terribly sweet.

I put my hand to my mouth.
The audience turns around.
They are watching the wrong one.

One of us is double,
One of us original.

She blows a kiss, takes off her wig
so they'll know who is who,
which is which.

Dr. Kris: Interpreting Dreams

No.

I am walking over the stones and monuments.
I feel the cool stone and then the grass
on my bare feet.
Grass and then stone,
stone and grass.

I am dancing naked over the gravestones.
There is no feeling, just the wet dew on my skin
and the fluid motion of the dance at night
over the gravestones.

I stand up naked, everyone looks.
I walk down the aisle while the minister
goes on preaching.
Everyone smiles,
everyone loves me. And I know I am doing
the right thing.

After Arthur
Payne-Whitney Clinic
Winter 1961

After Arthur, they said, they promised
I would get my memory back
if only there was one thing
I could grasp—

a spar in a river,
a cloud attached to the sky,
the taste of snow.

Before the car shot off the road
like a homing planet,

before the accident I expected,

there were white paper flags
tied to the grasses.

They waved and waved their
message.

When I drew near,
they were mist and frost,
silent.

But behind that field, in the woods,
you drew a bead on a target.
As the stag went down its eyes met yours—

after all,
you were the closest life to it.

(What evil flowers are in my room,
brought by someone
with a snow-blank face,
no name.)

In my nightmare,
that moment after the flagged grasses,
I saw you crouch,
the bullet struck as the deer stepped
out.

I saw nothing.
I saw the car aim itself,
then I heard screaming.

If there is a hell,
that scream has an origin.

I was lucky this time.
It wasn't my turn.

Do I weep for a stranger then?
Do I weep for a husband?

Why am I in this white bed,
my skin, hair, my voice
a vanishing froth,

as if I had gone
missing?

What was the name again?

Arthur.
Your last husband.

In My Own Words

I compromised
by dreaming of attracting
someone's attention
(besides God),

of having people look at me
and say my name.

They saw themselves
and condemned me,

they white-masked themselves
and blackened me.

I am part of nature.

How could they hate me?

For Clark Gable

Even though I prick the capsules with a pin
to speed the effect,

this is not suicide,
it is an answer.

Clark Gable—they say I caused your death.

Your wife,
your unborn child
begin a funeral feast to which

I am uninvited.

You, a dead god,
unresurrected,
what is your wish?

This room, this drug
lead to
indecision at the window,

my foot on the ledge,
curtains billowing white...

did you mean to be alone,
did you mean me not to join you?

The Dress

I know that dress.
It is my dress, meant for me.
Not just the way it looks from the back—

that dress is my flag.
A girl said, 'I would like to look like that,'
a man was struck dumb.

I belong to myself
in that dress,

my life wraps around me.

Then a woman in white brushes my hair back,
brushes the blood away
(it is an accident to which no one but me comes).

She says, 'Isn't it a shame to have to cut
the dress away, such a pretty dress,
a heavenly dress.'

Yes, I know what it means.
Success has its price.

Like Aimee Semple McPherson,
Of Los Angeles,
when they thought she had drowned,

but she had just run away with a man.

Best Wishes

*Best wishes for your early recovery
signed
From the man you tried to see nearly ten years ago
God forgive me.*

Dear father,

I have forgotten who I once hoped
you were.

You have less substance than my dark angel.

Too late. Too late.

I don't want to know when you die
(you are dying now, didn't you know?).

After Arthur Left

After Arthur left
I found I liked men.

There was a Sheik,
a driver,
a masseur.

Frank Sinatra used to keep me in his bedroom.

What else do you want to know?

I like soup,
pasta,
chocolate pudding;

and the Kennedys.

The palmist says I'm going to be
First Lady.

Happy Birthday, Mr. President
May 1962

I should know about omens by now,
be brave,
read the signs.

The lighting crew throws a spotlight
on empty space.

Should I have refused the moment?
Or stepped out (as I did)
in flesh absolute,
a glitter
of shape,
nothing beneath that a breath of wind
couldn't obliterate.

It was the champagne feeling
of déjà vû,
of everything over at the beginning.

I came in like a goddess
to men empty of dreams,

and fell into their whirlwind,
a desert that swallowed father and mother,
all history.

Be brave
(the dress is sheer silk soufflé),

and say to the President of the whole United States:

Happy birthday!
You and I are on intimate terms
with eternity.

Red Stockings

I met Bobby
At the Lawford's.
We went outside,
the beach like a silver spoon,
then lightning,
rain on top of drought,
then the floods—

I couldn't get home,
roads blocked,
water rising.

Bobby, stay with me, stay.

We held hands,
he let me see the whole world
of life and death.

He said:

they were running Trujillo in Dominica,
they were running the Bay of Pigs.

I wrote it down in a small red book.

Is this the secret, Bobby,
is this one it?

I knew about Hoover, the F.B.I.
Hoffa, the Teamsters,

but which one mattered?

I was wearing new red stockings:

Bobby liked me,
legs on fire,
the right length
from heel to thigh.

I mentioned the diary,
I said I thought my phone was tapped,

and he didn't call back.

Bobby, save me.
Bobby, you've got to get me out.

One doctor puts a pill in my mouth,
and another takes it out.

My mother sends
a smoke signal of warning.

But I'm drowning, drowning.

Bobby, why am I so alone,
lost, waiting for you
wearing new red stockings?

This is My House, Spring 1962

Come in.
This is my house.
The only house I'll ever own.
This is my home.

A Spanish-type hacienda
with a garage,
a guest house....

What was it Christ said?
About knowing the vine?
My religion is simple—
do good and love others.

It doesn't say how.
It doesn't say you shouldn't.

This is my house.
Though I find out after the fact,
it has been wired up, bugged—

every voice is recorded,
every act.

Am I that important?
It's like having God,
or a father and mother.

This is my house.
I am making a life in it.

I have
Joe, of course,
and...

everyone comes to my house.

I have a woman to clean and cook.
She is a spy
but it doesn't matter
since I know this.

I want people to be interested.
I want to be watched.

I am thirty-six years old.
I'm the one with two scars on her body.

I could call you.
I could make you happy.

Let me give, give.

Eunice, my housekeeper, has come back in the car.
She has bought steak and champagne for dinner.
Eunice is—I don't know. I pay her.
I pay all the bills.

She checks to see I've taken all my pills,
makes sure they go down.

Everything has gone wrong, wrong!

What did I say?

This is my house.
My name is Marilyn.
I am divorced.

It is Saturday night.
Who shall I call?

Hello?

Hello, baby.
Don't you remember me?

Who is this?

Can't you guess?

If you would only tell me....

A long time ago. I lent you money.

What did you say your name was?

We met at a party. And I ....

I'll send a cheque.

I knew you weren't like the others, you're accessible, right?

I'm just like anybody.

Marilyn, do you want to....

This is my house.
It is everything I ever wanted.
I can bring my friends here,
I'm going to Mexico to buy furniture.

I was born...
now I'm walking through a valley....

I'm going to buy dishes.
I took nothing from the marriages
but jelly glasses.

They remind me I can keep on
going.

Except
now I've got this house,
with flowers, a swimming pool—

someday I'm going to learn to use it.

If you felt water rising,
what would you do?

Under the studio lights
I see my mother.
Her body is thick
as a page of print,
I mean real, every time there's a flaw
in my performance.

She has moved into the closet,
now she comes out, in smoke,

but this is my body,
my house.

Whether the door to the house is black or not,

the house is white.
Sharp rocks hold the house up.
The blue sea is mandatory.

Roses climb the steps and scratch an entrance.
There is one face, two,
a quick cat.

A dim pink hallway,
a table pushed against the wall,
a radio shaped like a bread box.

Nothing moves but the violets
inching at light.

The house is white,
primary,
empty.

The Dressing Room, August 4-5, 1962

The same sun,
the same earth
in the tall mirrors.

My double holds her two selves
in her four hands. We wear
black silk toreador pants,
a print silk blouse, our hair
a super-heated platinum—

the same sun,
the same earth
binds us.

One holds her breasts up,
one turns and displays her buttocks.

There is no crying, no sadness
in the room of mirrors.
Whatever we see
is the body constant, reliable.
It decorates, simplifies.

We work on it and then
all the work is undone.

I like to look in the mirror.
It means
nothing holds
nothing.

No bra, no panties,

one layer of colour like the atmosphere.

One body, one flesh, one spirit,
the self with the self combined:

luminosity,
double light rising and setting
all at once.

This is the last room I visit
in life.
See it as it is then.

Where are her blue dresses?
No blue dresses? She always liked blue.
But that dress, formless, on a hanger
will do.

The mortician receives it,
then a slip,
a brassière,

and I'm dressed as though I'd never
been free in life.

Three husbands, not too many, just enough.

One to spin the thread of life,
one to measure it,
one to cut.

Jim, Joe, Arthur....

I dreamed that my nipples

were turned inside out,
inverted, shallow-pitted cups.

I wanted them pointed—
everything I believed in
depended on it.

They are the marks, the stigmata
of who I am.

I struggled to turn them right side out.
Oh, it hurt,

but what did that count,
I had an end in mind,
I was going to be
woman.

First one, then the other stood up—
they were a kind of success,
they were about to signify,

they were covered in blood.

But no one wants to see the pain,

you have to pretend...

(an unreal doll, hair blond as
a Siberian wind,

crying love me, love me,

drink my milk
and never thirst again).

They came to look

at a crypt small as a bug box,
at my last brass-doored house.

A walled garden, a small chapel,

a lawn dotted with headstones.

In the walls are burials, layer on layer.

The alcoves have names: Sanctuary of Love,
Sanctuary of Peace—

I am in the Corridor of Memories.

There are always flowers and messages.
See? Read this:

*Marilyn, when you died all the light went
out of the world.*

Sunshine falling over the walls like broken glass.
Inside, enclosed, safe.

GRANDFATHER WAS A SOLDIER

To
*A Soldier of the Great War
Known Unto God*

Sailed from Montreal per S.S. Scandinavian, 17th of June 1915

✧

All of the dead are handsome
and young, and some
like you were tanned by Ontario sun, arms hard
as iron rods
from keeping the horse to the plough.
Sometimes, your brother said, they made you
take the harness. I promise you

the land has since turned to Eden.
Where there were stones
and flint, chalk,
the charred bark of limbs, sky
that fell and never lifted
for four years,

are now neat fields of cabbage, lettuce and wheat;
red-brick houses with white trim,
chickens and pigs browsing together in meadows,
a few sheep. Cattle drink from the shell holes.

The land is rich and fertile with a few
irregular hills.

Reasons? For this journey?
The sound of artillery in dreams.
A few brown photographs.
A silence two generations old.

The countryside is rolling green patchwork
Stop near Abbéville where the road
diverges from the River Somme: a belt
of thick green shows its path.
North to Bailleur and Ploegsteert.

Through 'Plug Street' to St. Eloi.
See craters from the great mine
explosions there.

To Ypres.

June 27, 1915　　　　*Attached from 52nd Battalion*
June 29, 1915　　　　*Transferred to 32nd Reserve Battalion C.E.F.*
August 20, 1915　　　*4 days pay overstaying leave*
August 28, 1915　　　*Transferred to 3rd Battalion, France*
August 29, 1915　　　*Taken on strength 3rd Battalion, France*
September 4, 1915　　*Joined the 3rd Battalion in Flanders*

Flanders. The rains begin.

◆

Just north of Hill 62 and the Mount Sorrel memorial
is the small private museum of Sanctuary Wood.
It has been kept by the Schuyère family—grandfather to
grandson—since the Great War.
The current proprietor, who is tall and heavily built, sits idly,
overflowing a stool, at the counter of the café that is attached
to the museum.
Behind him is a clock made entirely of brass bullets and
shell casings.
It is about five feet tall and two and a half feet wide.
It does not work.

At the beginning of the War grandfather Schuyère was evacuated
to Poperinge and grandmother to France. But afterwards,

when they returned to a countryside grey with mud,
trench lines swollen with rats, barbed wire, unexploded shells—
even early in 1919—the old soldiers had begun to return too.

50

At first Monsieur Schuyère acted as a guide,
locating the exact intersection of trenches where
someone had lost a limb
or a friend,

where the 'during' part of before and after, that now made
up their lives, had occurred.
And then, observing that a future might be made of this,

and noting the speed with which the plough and Nature conspired
to disguise the landscape,
he bought a piece of the ridge that had been Sanctuary Wood
and began to collect shells, boots, shreds
of uniforms, helmets,
an aeroplane engine and wooden
propeller, pistols, several Lee Enfield rifles, a hated Ross (its
stock from long burial was the texture of leather),

and glass plate photographs to be viewed in stereoscope,
housed in rectangular wooden boxes (1 franc).

>   Image one: the man shown on the glass slide
>   lies wrapped in a blanket on a table.

His breast is white, fleshy and bare.
His eyes are alive, intelligent,
disassociated from what the camera shows
lying inches below them:
the threads of flesh and sinew holding
head to
torso.
Below the nose—a gaping bristle of meat,
no mouth or jaw, the wound patterned
with the white stitch of maggots.

>   Image two: in a tree—the head and forelegs
>   of a horse.

The hooves hang neat as gloves,
one crossed over the other, a foot or two above
the ground.
the nostrils are flared, the head

larger than the tree trunk that has been scraped clean
by fire.
In a second tree,
draped over a branch like a tea cloth, is a man, complete
except for one hand.
He is abandoned there
as after a flood.

Language fails, as you knew it would, lacks evidence
of touch.

◆

In the café the proprietor lights a fire in the cast iron stove
to cheer his visitor who has come in out of the cold
twilight July rain.
Together they listen to white Belgian doves,
unsettled and restless in the weather,
alight and gather and
fly to and from the wooden roof
and the heavy, vigorous, gusty trees that have grown
out of the ashes of the old forest.

Outside, the fenced-off trenches are filling with water and mud.
They have not altered since 1918 although a pale green frosting
of moss and weed seeps over the original waste ground.
Rusted curlique stakes mark the path of barbed wire between the lines,

and a field telephone wire remains strung from charred tree
to tree suggesting incomplete messages.

It is wet, the woods, moss, stones, bush, are familiar.
Several broken tombstones, from a cemetery begun by the Germans
in 1916 when in brief possession of the Wood,
lie next to a pile of lichen-stained bones.

Inside the café the visitor imagines for a moment
that two sturdy elderly figures have entered the warm circle
of the fire.

He is, of course, mistaken,
although the more he thinks,
the more he believes he can hear impossible things,

such as his own dead grandfather's cough
(who was a soldier here)

and the drop and spatter of a cuckoo's egg
on soft grass.

✧

> Image: he feels a strange skin wrapping over his own.
>
> Image: the trenches are overlooked by hills, the men
> easy targets in their pitiful marshy blinds.

✧

Mire and pooled water.
Two soldiers carry the white wrapped lower half
of a man.
They have strapped him onto a bar
(as water carriers would) between them.
They have made him a seat and toe rest,

although there is nothing to him above waist level.

A group of dead men are lying on the ground.
But, propped up against another,
one man has his hands over his eyes and may therefore
be alive.

> Rickshaws, pulled by one man each,
> carrying one body each, in a long line that stretches
> far back into the photograph.

There are screens alongside the roads the men march on.
They are supposed to hide their movements from enemy artillery.
The screens appear to be torn silk
or rice paper.

        A row of mud-covered dead soldiers laid out
        in front of a church altar.

A horse, wound free, but its slack sticky belly
covered with flies.

        As commonplace as kindling

lies the upper body of a man.
He has a wide-eyed, delicate, high-cheekboned face,
wavy hair, and his fine hands
are upraised.

And now, gunshots in the fields,
two at five-second intervals,

to frighten crows from the ripening corn.

December 29, 1915   *Influenza. Admitted to 2nd Canadian Field*
                                    Ambulance.
January 8, 1916   *Rejoined Unit.* [1]

                ◇

It has rained heavily all night.
The visitor walks up the path to Mount Sorrel.

        Here at Mount Sorrel and on the line from Hooge to St. Eloi
        the Canadian Corps fought in the defence of Ypres.
        April - August, 1916 [2]

From here he can see, looking eastwards, peaceful farmfields,
a line of trees, fences,
more thickly wooded slopes in the distance.

The memorial area is planted with red roses.

To the west the fields slope away to Ypres,
its church spires visible through the mist.

Black and white cows sway in the meadow.

Behind the holly hedge M. and Mme. Schuyère are waking up.
They hear the steps of the visitor as he passes by
on the concrete walk and opens the brass door
that is set in a stone wall of the enclosure.

Inside the door is a register of the dead.

The visitor wants something in writing
to take him through the maze of battlefields,

although he has not noticed the Schuyères
or the ghostly presence of his grandfather
who has taken up position at his shoulder.

It has begun to rain again.
To the south the meadows are brilliant green,
and a few farm horses stalk quietly along wet furrows.

The young man opens the book,
and reads the first entry:

Pitoyables les conséquences.

(Twin gun shots sound. A salute? A warning?)

The grandson closes the book and puts it away in its niche
in the wall.
The garden is bordered with low bushes of salal, briar rose,
and freesia. There is laburnum and substantial maple.
He notices that his footsteps leave a clear print
in the heavily dewed grass.
Lilac and red currant block his path.
Red roses, as in a tea garden.

The noise of a tractor starting up fills the morning.

I leave this note
beside you while you are sleeping.

It is my Will.

Everything not crossed out is
what I wanted to say.

       Image: men hauling artillery through waist deep mud,
       uphill.

An airship hangs like a child's cloud-drawing
over the trenches.

Craters, stones, chalk,
pieces of wood, of bodies: a leg with a boot,
a curve of waist.

Dead boy in the foreground.
A man, stomach opened, bones
showing white in his chest,
alive.

      ✧

Craters 1-7 are in the St. Eloi fields; [3]
but each is filled with green water
at which a cow gazes.
In which did he drop a bayonet,
in which find the helmet with a death's head on it?

Only the slick scar on his right arm
and the deep cough that keeps him awake in the winter
are lasting souvenirs.

There is also the hard work of not thinking,
not telling the children
the lessons,

turning away from the self when it sickens,
leaving wounds to fester or heal,

taking each breath shallowly,
telling no one
and hoping something will come of it,
someone's luck.

Old M. Schuyère is lost.
Disconsolately he toes a hole in the loose ground
at the end of a row of beets.
All around him industrious farm labourers
are filling in the holes of the landscape.

From each bucket of earth, each pail of dung that
they empty,
spring vivid green shoots.

Soon all that is visible is smoothly surging
pasture.

M. Schuyère has uncovered an ancient rusted compass.
He is pleased with his find and
following its direction, walks blindly south

and climbs to the mouth of a giant crater.
It is the largest on the Western Front…

he peers into its moonscape and sees
bees and a few scarlet and black butterflies among the stones.
On the rim where he stands, his feet are caught in a tangle
of blackberry canes.

There is a fine view from his vantage point.

*This land has
Been Privately
Purchased as a Permanent Memorial
to the Men who Fought in the
Battle of the Somme 1916....This Land is Dangerous.*

M. Schuyère
becomes aware of the golden virgin of Albert on a church tower
in the distance.
He modestly averts his gaze and finds

wreaths of pale plastic poppies lying like bitter berries
in the weeds.

Interdit: Cette terre est sacrée.

*The Canadian Corps bore a valiant part in forcing back
the Germans on these slopes during the Battles of the
Somme, September 3rd - November 18th 1916.*

Object: To capture Candy Trench, the Sugar Factory
and 1500 yards of Sugar Trench in front of Courcelette.

I stood at the junction of
Jam Row and Sugar Trench.
It was noon
and flies buzzed like bullets
around my face.

The wall was head height
and I looked at the poisoned land
beyond Sugar
until summer flowers climbed like angels
round the wraiths of smoke,

and I knew
others were still caught in the grass,

but I heard them coming
hands, arms, legs, weapons muffled

in Jam Row near the junction with Sugar.

✧

September 7, 1916   *Gun shot wound in right arm.* [4]

✧

A French peasant cycles past the entrance to the Courcelette Memorial:
ivy, shade and sunlight,
holly, maple, salal;

and continues on down the Sunken Road from the Sugar Factory
to Courcelette Village.

A tractor, like a black cat, crosses his path
and disappears over the rolling downs of barley
and potatoes.

The grandfather-soldier, who has at first walked ahead,
begins to lag behind in the heat.
He is irritated, as he looks at the fields, that he cannot recognise
any landmarks.
A thousand tiny black insects stray from the air
onto his skin and clothing,
and he watches his grandson mirror his actions
in brushing them away.

He spits—uncharacteristically—
just missing the shoe of M. Schuyère
who has taken off his jacket and is looking for a spade
with which to lift potatoes.

But this is the Somme and there are 1777 unidentified dead
in one field's small cemetery...plus
Adanac, Regina Trench, Mouquet Farm.

Imagine the first ploughing—metal, wire, stone—
and the first growth...
a snail crawls over the back of a gravestone.

The ghostly folowers begin to lose shape
as they are engulfed in an atmosphere
of fresh harvest.

For the grandson walking becomes more difficult.
It is as though he pulls a long chain including
not only the Schuyères
and his grandfather,
but a thousand others.

Their legs sink in the capacious earth,

but he pulls and they, smiling, are carried along.

Mme Schuyère starts a song:

Brave lads Thou didst hear the call
while shirkers stayed at home.
Thy gallant lives
we could ill spare
to lose across the foam.

M. Schuyère is embarrassed but no one else
minds what Madame sings:
it is only a song to march to.

This could be a perfect summer evening
if the sun holds to its westerly course,
and the skylark's descent to the field
and the dropping wind coincide;

60

if all things remain on schedule,
winding down. The tall grass beside the
River Avre leans against the soft mud bank
and thistles thrive and rushes bend
and rise and

all the world, the sky with a flush of clouds,
is nodding a still, tuneless harmony:

a red train draws a line across the horizon,
a jet opens the belly of the sky

and all the unspoken thought that lies in you,
warmed all day in the wheat stubble where men die,
subsides.

Men die and women descend from windows
as widows and die too,

that being all the possibilities.
One way or another, it works
and where we are, in between, means waiting
along the perfect horizon of the river

for the evening mist to fall
and the morning mist to rise
and reveal the 'final objective'.

Between then and now is the night,
another turning from coolness to warmth,
rubbing the two cool stones of our bodies
until something comes alive between them,
white and vivid as a nova, burning out
in the reflection of the river where
all a long summer our grandfathers drank
a miracle, harvesting at last
a war's conclusion.

There, nothing decided,
we choose each word of love,
laying stepping stone after slippery
stepping stone.

✧

*Those to whom the fortunes of war denied the known
and honoured burial given to their comrades in death*

have their names inscribed on the stone pillars of Thiepval. [5]

There are so many names
that every one who visits finds
his own
and that of his father
and his father's brothers,
distant cousins
and second cousins twice removed

who may or may not be members of his
mother's family.

The register of the missing is in sixteen volumes.

M. Schuyère adjusts a sign—*Danger of falling brick*—

so that the grandson can approach the writing closely enough
to discover his name for himself
and find community *in absentia.*

The ghostly chain joins up with other comrades
and they roll like children downhill
to the German lines and the emplacements at Beaumont Hammel. [6]

Some surviving instinct of caution stops them
at the precipice of Y ravine. They look back
and note that they have passed the
Tree of Death:

it stands upright, forked, leafless
in no-man's land;

and they let go and drop out of sight into the hidden cradle
of the north wind.

But the soldier-grandfather has caught his uniform sleeve
on the tree, and his grandson is rooted beside him
lighting a cigarette.

Someone calls a name
from the bottom of the ravine

and the old soldier shifts his attention
to an inscription on the black petrified trunk:

New armies.
Pals and chums Together.
A lesson in Duty.
Never Forgotten;

a cross made of popsicle sticks,
a sun-bleached velvet poppy for its heart.

A family is crossing the battlefield. Mother and daughter
peer into the green trenches. A little boy, wearing fluorescent socks,
jumps in. They are all learning lessons.

The grandson is occupied with personal problems
and soon falls asleep at the foot of the tree.

The soldier begins to suffer from his festering arm wound
and lies down
and waits for the stretcher bearers to come.

Sun over the Valley of the Somme.
The grain is harvested,
the cabbages plump as Christmas puddings.
The wide slow river is hedged with
ash and hazel-wand.
A barge slides along the surface of the water.

How can I tell you what it was like
knowing I had to go back,
knowing what was ahead.

Father in heaven / we bow to Thy will / But O for a sound / of a voice that is still.

✧

November 17, 1916   Discharged military hospital
November 24, 1916   6 weeks P. T.
March 6, 1917   To 12th Reserve Battalion
April 21, 1917   Transferred to 3rd Battalion
April 22, 1917   Arrived in France
April 28, 1917   Arrived 3rd Battalion in field

✧

The soldier-grandfather shakes with ague in the chalk tunnels below Vimy Ridge. [7]

Perhaps it is the nearness of the German lines.
They are only a crater away from the entrance.
Perhaps it is because the others who went forward whole and returned wounded (the tunnel forks so that the fresh troops cannot see them) refuse to show themselves.
In this place he is as ignorant as his grandson.

He can scarcely breathe.
The old wound in his lung where the bullet sits
shortens his breath.

His grandson keeps close behind the guide
who can take him through the maze safely.
The guide explains the rusted weapons and implements
that are stacked along the sides of the tunnel.
Only the guide is not aware of the cold. The tunnels stretch
behind the lines for over a mile.

He lights a cigarette
but it goes out as there is not enough oxygen in the tunnel
to support a flame.

His hands shake. He is closer to fear than he has been
since the War.
The tunnels are too clean. Without passion,
he thinks,
there cannot be courage or love.

He relaxes.

He understands that he has been waiting
for the appearance of rats, but that now, incorporeal,
he does not need to fear them.

His grandson is flirting with the female guide
who smiles kindly as he says everything that previous visitors
have said before.

Nothing in the tunnels is new.
Everything has been left as it was: a network of pickaxed
chalk roads six feet high, strung with wire for telephones
and lights, water pumps. You are safe here from shells

until you go back up, as you must,
to finish the tour.

>   I am seated (reflects the grandson) in the same field
>   my grandfather's battalion crossed
>   on its way to take Farbus Wood. To my right
>   is the Commandant's house,
>   behind me, behind the tractor and cows,
>   is the village of Thélus.

The soldier-grandfather sitting behind him nods and takes a bite
of the chocolate that the grandson absentmindedly laid down
in the grass. Sweat pours down his arms
and he pushes up the heavy sleeves of his uniform.

There is little sun, but heavy cumulus clouds blanket and heat
the sky.

To the south is Arras. The Thélus village clock strikes One.

To the left is a field of chard and next to that is golden wheat.
A skylark flutters around the grandfather's head.
The grandson brushes flies away from his face, continuing to eat,
waiting for something to happen.

What does he expect?

The grandson considers the nature of 'home'.

He traces the path of the attack in reverse
and comes to a memorial to his grandfather's Division.

Another walk, another cemetery.
At Bois Carré he finds
the grave of Pte. W. A. Nickerson
accidentally killed on 4th June 1919.

Accidentally?

He examines the tombstones for messages:

> *Under the sod*
> *receive our treasure*
> *To rest in God*
> *waiting his pleasure.*

    Jump-off:

swath of black field,
chalk and flint stones,
a foot's breadth of camomile….

    On this side the ridge is a morass
    of mud and shell craters.
    On the other are the untouched farms of the fertile
    Douai Plain.

...rise up the slope to the right of the village,
crescent sweep past the Commandant's house
then down into Farbus Wood.

The machine-guns, in concrete emplacements
at the head of the wood,
fire uphill at the running soldiers.

Brambles, nettles as high as a man,
cow pats,
grassed over shell-hole traps,
cattle and warm straw where the guns fired

at forgotten names:

    Quinn, Wright, Forest, James,

*The trial is hard / I will not complain / But trust in God /
to meet again.*

    Perrin, Swyze, Charbonneau, Hall, Hamilton, Bullock.

Grandfather stands above and looks over emptiness.
Grandfather considers sacrifice.

Mme and M. Schuyère are just cresting the ridge.
Puffing for breath, they have no time for conversation

but continue to draw near
and together reflect on
the invention of armour.

Thunderheads roll and clap like allies.

M. Schuyère and his wife rub their sore feet.
The weather has turned hot and humid, the sun burning
out of the south all day.
They are northerners. They do not appreciate thirst.

The old woman pulls her scarf over her head.
She has been here before, during the War.
She knows how to get a loaf of bread anywhere.
M. Schuyère, she thinks,
has never appreciated her skills.

After coming down from Vimy (where they were lost in the woods
for several hours, though M. Schuyère denies this saying
he has an instinct for direction), they rest at La Targette.

Everything changes over the years,
but the old couple sit together and M. Schuyère opens the brass door
and takes the visitors' book from its niche.

He is lucky and has arrived ahead of the others
in time to remove a mistaken message.

Relationships are as complex as a landscape, he thinks.
But that is the problem when people die young and their offspring
grow old before them.

Mme Schuyère can read and she insists on examining
the page before it is removed from the book.
Indeed, it has been written by a General.

General P.C. Cook DSO MC KBE Oak Meadow,
Kingston-upon-Thames

All these sanctimonious expressions in this book—look!
These chaps were <u>called</u> [the word is heavily underscored]
into the army and went—reluctantly. They did not give
their life 'for king and country' their life was taken from them—
violently—let us not go giving semi-illiterate boys
of 18 or 19 attributes of nobility and self-sacrifice in death which
we'd not have given them in life—
those who returned were unable to make a living—
and most spent their lives in the abject poverty of the 20's—
these kids buried here had never drunk a beer
[Madame exclaims at this] *never slept with a woman*
[the old couple smile at each other]

68

some had never taken a bath in their life
as the sub-standard housing they came from
did not include such luxuries
[the old couple pass over this uncomprehendingly]—

the best sentiment is 'These Poor Bastards'.

Madame herself strikes the match and fires the paper. Then
she replaces her shoes and stockings,
and rests.

The visitor's page is blank;

except for the evidence
of a dead rat
on the cemetery lawn.

We sleep face to face
close as enemies in the tent.
Beneath us a field of clover,
above us a tower of bones
hollow as this tunnelled hill.

We sleep face to face,
but you have taken the bayonet
out of its rusty case.
It is not easy
to slide it in from behind
at the base of the spine
through the motor nerves.
You watch the eyes of your enemy age
and change to those of a woman.
Each act of killing is another caress
until you are ashamed.

We sleep face to face on top of a ridge
of bones. From the height of the tower

the countryside falls away in a mist
of villages.
Each one is a story
with a set of graves.

You stir the body—like making a cake,
it is against sun direction—
the batter resists the movement
and still the eyes will not turn away
but search you out.

Even slitting its throat fails,
though it begins to look grateful.

At last, having pity on it / her,
you reach in with your stained hands
and pull the windpipe out.
Never again
will she accuse
nor will you search among bones
for an omission of sins.

Outside the ossuary where the bones
of 30, 000 unknown dead reside
are old soldiers wearing black berets.
Everything is forbidden: smoking, dogs, bicycles.
Ne Parlez Pas. [8]

All night the young man has dreamed
of marriage to a beautiful young woman.
He has forgotten his grandfather
in this tomb of strangers.

The cavern is tiled like a Byzantine church.
At one end a top layer of coffins lies exposed
like biscuits in a tin.

He climbs the stairs.

In a glass case of relics he finds

a photograph of Farbus Wood,
the watch of a Canadian soldier,
men digging buried treasure
out of the bottom of a Souchez trench,
a photograph of bones belonging to 16,000 men.

He climbs another staircase and another

and another until, out of breath, using his arms to push
against the narrowing walls of the tower,
he finds himself at the top
looking out over the wheat and corn fields
far past the sprays of white crosses to the dim line
of distant cities.

On each exit door he has passed is a sign:
Do not open. Danger of death.

✧

July 10, 1917   To hospital
July 21, 1917   Rejoined Unit

✧

The attack on Hill 70 is delayed by bad weather and is set for 15 August. [9]

✧

A family leaves its car
and walks across the parking lot
to the Supermarché. In a few moments they reappear
eating ice-cream, and sit on the curb together
eyeing their surroundings.

They cannot speak to each other
because of the noise of air conditioners
and the music which booms loud as a god's voice
over the squashed top of the short-legged hill.

Beside the parking lot is an old chalk quarry.
Its bare sides have sprouted with camomile;
the healing plant's pale yellow breath is spread
like a memory of mustard gas
over the bruised land.

White daisies, lumps of chalk, toilet paper,
a broken dish in the nettles, long grass pushing aside
small-bore stones.

Over 3500 casualities fell here
on the short-cut between the trailer park
and shopping centre

and further down where cub aeroplanes practise-fly.

The lines of advancing infantrymen extended
for two miles.

The family finishes its treat and returns home
to Lens.

A delivery truck arrives
and deposits a pyramid of tins.

    North...

The land is gentle and rolling.

    To Ypres, through the Menin gate, along the canal
    to Potijze.

From Gravenstafel Ridge look south to Ypres' broken towers...
and north-east across the unspeakable valley of corpses
to Passchendaele.

Bloated, gaseous flesh in a cauldron of mud.
Men are left to drown
like maimed fish.

There is no drinking water
but a grey rat appears
wearing a red collar with silver bell.

*The Canadian Corps in October-November 1917
advanced across this valley then a treacherous morass,
captured and held the Passchendael Ridge.* [10]

Cost: 15,654

Something was making me cry
and couldn't stop.

If only I could have slept—
but there was piteous screaming

and cold hail as a man
ripped the curtain back.

If I could break
into a dream of sweet language—

but his eyes are wise,
and once open

the living won't take him back.

Old M. Schuyère enters the memorial garden
where Crest Farm once stood—500 yards from the church—
with his wife. They come here every evening at sunset
on their journey back and forth through the Salient and Somme. It has
been a long day.
Both peasants take their shoes off and rub their sore feet.

A cyclist goes by with radio playing.

M. Schuyère shakes his head and Madame
clucks her disapproval. They look around suspiciously
before relaxing on the stone steps in front of the monument, looking
westwards over the fields of corn.

Just in front and to the right of them
is the niche that contains the book of visitors.
M. Schuyère and his wife have never signed—
this is not their village.

From behind the holly hedge they are being watched.
It has stopped raining and the sun
is bright and hot. The pages of the visitors' books
are still warm with handling.
Someone has written of the memorial
that 'it is a disgrace!'
The Schuyères shift uncomfortably on the stone steps
as if they could read this for themselves.
Someone coughs in the bushes near them,
but they take no note.

It is the cough of a man who has breathed chlorine
and mustard gas.
Even now, as he sits in the gorse border,
he senses the seared surfaces of his internal organs.
He looks away from the Schuyères

out over the westward plain that
he crossed on foot with the army.
Where a red brick house stands, horses nibbling at hay
by the fence, was Vine Cottage.
He had returned from convalescence to fight there.

It was nothing he would speak of, even if he could,
although the name has been passed
down through generations like a code.

Passchendaele.

✧

He refuses to look below the undulating green countryside
to what he had known. Instead he regards his grandson
who has signed the guest book minutes before the arrival
of the Schuyère couple, and who feels more at peace
than he has for many months.

Good farms, the grandson thinks. Good wind,
the smell of roses. He is at peace because
all the work has been done.

He brushes the hair from his forehead
as if brushing away a sign,

and remembers at what age his grandfather fought here:
in November 1917 his grandfather was twenty-three,
younger than himself now.

The grandson scratches at his upper lip
as if he had once worn a moustache.

He has eaten lunch that day in the square at Ypres,
not far from the Menin Gate,
and has crumbs of bread on his clothing.
He brushes them off.
A dead man pays no attention to such details, he thinks,

and leans back against the sun warmed step
only to start and hurry down the north path
as the cyclist with the radio goes by
and the couple Schuyère
come to the end of their wanderings
for the day.

For them it has been successful. They have unearthed
two shells from the roadworks of the new motorway
that will cross the old trench line between Polygon
and Nonnesboschen Woods. Madame Schuyère has come up
with the idea of threading bullet casings on chains
and selling them to tourists.

"They're made of good brass," she says. "It's not as if they
won't get something for the money." But she lowers
her eyes under the stern gaze of M. Schuyère.

The new bullets go back to their manufacturer.

The fields that are green today were once bleached white
with gas. The tear wet eyes of Mme Schuyère examine them
as if regretting a clean laundry; although

no one has made a fortune here but the farmers
who like the especially rich soil.

The soldier-grandfather falls in step with his grandson
who is ready to leave Passchendaele village.
He thinks of the few moments of quiet
when there was wind in the trees
and a warm sun.
At this moment the grandson is aware
of the gentle pressure of a soldier's hand
on his shoulder.

Hill 60 [11]

Cratered, long brown grass
fringes the bowl.
Sheep step over concrete
and iron rods; the emplacements,
a bunker deep in the hill,
are used by rabbits.

Beneath, the dead creep quietly as bats,
setting charges for the future.
Each footfall makes them hesitate
and give watch
from view holes underground.

Each soldier waits
to gain advantage over each other
and wire up the mines.

A train passes along the embankment
to Shrapnel Corner. It carries men back
to their holes in the ramparts of Ypres
where there are rats as big as prairie gophers,

where old wounds ache and the next grow ripe
for the bullet's lance.

✧

January 6, 1918   *Attended Corps Gas School*
January 19, 1918   *Rejoined Unit*

✧

Crucifix Corner is bounded with a wall
and hornbeam hedge,
planted with poplar and lavender.

Sweet peas and mint straggling on the verge
tempt the passing herd of Charolais cattle.

Gone from our home / but not from our hearts.

✧

January 11, 1918   *Granted 14 days leave*
February 7, 1918   *Returned from leave*
March 1, 1918   *Appointed Lance Corporal*

✧

From Amiens,
down the hill into Boves, between rows of elm, past
the factory, through the town and across the deep ravine
of the Route Nationale.

As they cross the fields of cabbages together,
a red deer leaps away from their khaki shadows
into the depths of the wood.

Inside are the "fosses",
holes dug under roots into the chalk soil
where 26 years later twenty-seven bodies—
members of the Résistance—will lie...

...to Hangaard Wood in the first line of objectives,
footsteps echoing a thousand previous,
given no choice
but to set the world quaking:

the structure will fall and rise
as have all towers of endeavour.

And these shades call to each other across the rustle
of unharvested wheat in mixed tongues,
but saying one thing—

that *this* was never intended.

The wind brings a swirl of black insects and falls away
leaving the utmost quiet.

Ahead is a row of spinning-top shrubs, and a single
injunction:

You who wish to show gratitude,
kneel down and pray
for my soul.

But this you will not do, out of pride and unbelief
and faith in your intentions.

The soft wind tingles the skin
and rolls over the hills and the vanished troops,

above the level of trees.

✧

> *The road to Villers-Bretonneux goes due North from the
> village of Demuin, up a steep hillside, and after a mile
> it passes between two portions of Hangaard Wood.
> In April 1918 the wood was at the junction of French
> and British forces defending Amiens, but it was cleared
> by the Canadian Corps on August 8.*
>
> *The cemetery there is enclosed by a brick wall
> and planted with Irish yews and flowering shrubs,
> and is in a sheltered position in agricultural land.*

A crow, frightened by the approach of the travellers,
flies into the sun.

The woods are edged with wild roses.

There are blue flowers and shell holes deep in the vegetation.

> *Toronto Cemetery commands extensive views
> and is isolated in a field between Demuin and Marcelcave.
> This enclosure is planted with crab apple
> and was begun on the first day of battle.*

Trembling white birds stand on long thin legs
in the roadway.

Two training jets make a low sweep
over the graveyards.

The enemy hides in shallow redoubts
in the wheat fields.
You hear nothing, but at least you've attained
higher ground.

Shell holes are scattered like petals from a single rose
across the chalk fields.

Pushing the enemy back towards the old front lines
of the Somme, deep into familiar territory,

pushing him back through corn and wheat
and cabbage, red poppies, across streams and walls ,
pushing ahead:

the bullet hits and bites deeply into the chest,

and you drop to earth...

...Overhead the sky rolls on,
wind piling up the early morning mist
into stacks of dark cloud.
There is thunder in the distance
and the lightning of artillery.

Now only the weather counts
and the lapse of time until you go home.

Two training jets make a low sweep over the graveyards.

An enemy doctor eases the pain.
He is about to leave when you ask for something more
(lying on your back in the salt froth that is your breath).
And he returns and puts something in your hands
that feels like happiness.

August 8, 1918 Gun shot wound to chest. [12]

The sky is lit with sheet lightning
yellow as butter, the air as thick
and soft as that with mist.
Along the slow River Luce three figures move
at a steady pace.
These walk the boundaries, a single light showing
for each fate.

Each night
the river opens her belly and out come
ducks, a white swan, myriads of fish,
and a man, dressed in black, with his boat.
He offers eventual meeting
with the boundary walkers,

though this evening
you have successfully hidden in the rushes
at the water's edge,

having come to drink
the water and the smooth deep stream of air.

Near trees appear as distant as church spires.

And because he is a man, the soldier thinks
he fits there, in control of machinery:
the harvester, a hoe, the rusted artillery in the bushes
near the great crater.

The landscape is fresh, green and ripe,
the progress of valley and river as relentless
and constant as love.

The orders alone have lost meaning;
advancing, retreating over the same ground,
digging in,
or routing the enemy from once-wheat fields
and woods, over and over.

How much he assumes
about those who watch over us,

since all the mind can say is: It couldn't
be for nothing,

and the cost bears some relation
to the achievement
and the achievement to what is desirable,

and there is reason to the restless activity in the fields
making up lost time along the Western Front

as if there is hope, even in such a place.

✧

At the Arc de Triomphe M. and Mme Schuyère rest.
They have come to the end of their journey
and have lost sight, possibly forever,
of the soldier-grandfather. He has left
his grandson to find his way home alone.

So much the better, Madame thinks, and leans back
against the tomb of the Unknown Soldier.
Monsieur sits quietly. The stories they have heard about Paris
are enough to keep them there, hesitant, forever,
but the familiar whinny of a horse causes Madame to stir.

She gets up and goes over to it, stepping around
the peacefully laid out form of the Unknown Soldier.
The horse nudges her hand for sugar
as the breeze riffles its mane.

✧

October 18, 1918   *Admission to Canadian General Hospital
Bramshott for invaliding to Canada*
December 29, 1918   *Sailed on "Araguaya"*
January 10, 1919   *Arrived in Canada*

✧

The account was to begin
with the whinny of a horse at dawn,
with the light rising,
and a great beast shuffling in the meadow
outside the tent, near as rain
or a heart-beat.

It was to continue with fields of sunflowers,
faces contoured in the uncertain light
as clouds shifted and slept and herded round
the soft sun. The vines ran straight across hillside
terraces into caves of treasure; always accompanied
by music. Dawn, a scale coloured in red rock
and gold, the air of a cool high plain
in the regions of the mountains.

The horses stumble up the high meadows
towards a fortress, a sacred place meant to be
the centre of the matter.

The flies matter more,
and the wet cold.

We separate, turn faces away, towards, in conjunction
with the sun, as though it is the centre,
and blindly view the sights that have cost
centuries of lives.

Even when the sunflowers and sun join
and the horse's whinny becomes the breath of the beast
outside the flimsy safety of the tent: even when
we know what we believe, the past and future have
proven their argument
against ours.

Experience cannot keep its single thread,
and a thousand dreams fail—
as does invaluable love—

but I know your face.

CALLING ALL THE WORLD

"For a few days, black and white, democrats and communists, republicans and royalists in all countries, islands and continents have one feeling, one language, one direction...one feeling of compassion for this little living being twirling helpless over our heads."

— *Stutgarter ZEITUNG*

November 3, 1957:

The world's second artificial satellite, Sputnik II, was launched successfully into orbit by Soviet scientists today, with a dog named Laika as passenger.

Western sources have determined that the launching took place at 2:32 a.m. Greenwich Mean Time from the Kazakhstan site used for Sputnik I. The Soviet announcement said that Sputnik II's passenger, an 11 pound female dog of an uncertain breed had withstood without harm the 17,895 Mph velocity required to put the satellite in orbit.

Russian scientist, Professor A.A. Blagonravov, affirmed in Moscow that Laika is safe, hinting that means had been provided to bring her back to earth. Although not impossible, this would be exceedingly difficult, and official Russian sources have made no such promise. But even if she lives for only a short time, her experiences may help keep the first human space voyagers alive.

In a related development, there has been no explanation of the absence of the dog's trainer, Mr. Alexei Folchakov, from the Moscow news conference. Rumour has linked Folchakov's disappearance to the timing of the launch. A reliable source says that Folchakov was "extremely attached to the dog" and had worked with it since its birth.

Professor Blagonravov has denied all knowledge of Alexei Folchakov's whereabouts.

The watch towers in the mountain villages,
the yellow brick pyramids of cities of the
dead,
thousands of miles of steppe,
goats, still as icons on the peaks of the
Caucasus;

the only movement in this land is the
shrinking of the great salt seas,
the crumbling white ledges of their shores,

the atom by atom rearrangement of crystals.

Laika: almost a ghost, as quickly, like light
itself, she crosses the earth.

She passes the Volga and Ural Rivers, over
feather-grasses and wheatstubble, through
herds of cattle, past a church, a school, the
asphalt sands below the ruins of ancient
towns...

for somewhere to the east of the Aral Sea, Mr.
Folchakov has stepped to the door of the
Baikonur Cosmodrome and called her.

Laika...

He has looked at the clear November night sky,
at the Pole star above him, at the Great and
Little Dogs.

At nothing but the blue-grey land of
Kazahkstan where a thin dusting of snow lifts
and blows on the northeast wind.

Laika...

Tamerlaine, Genghiz Khan, Alexander the Great.
Footprints, hoofbeats, caravans, settlements
of yurts...Laika's claws click on the tracks.

Like railway lines, like maps.

A light goes on in the office.
The doors of the dome spread open.
Folchakov and Laika blink as the concrete
eyelid contracts.
They shiver and listen to the music that
accompanies the beams of light.

Why warn you?
You do not know the language of our music.
With one root to the sun,
our tendrils drift and touch a sea of space
making sound in each degree.

See the herdsman conducting souls,
and Orion's dog following his master.
How many who travel the green-blue pastures,
and hear the lowing of cattle,
have sweet songs also.
But lost. Are lost.

We are a chorus of stars.
We stand in the bowl of the sky.
We spread to its rim like shards
of broken glass.

Like the light of broken lives.

Lost. All lost.

Liftoff...Sputnik II...November 3 at 2:32 GMT.
Velocity: 17,895 Mph...Passenger: 1 11-lb.
Experimental animal...Transmitting 200.05 and
400.002 megacycles.

✧

As they sped upwards, they travelled through
what appeared to be layers of sediment.

"The universe is not as we have been told,"
explained Mr. Folchakov, with his nose to the
capsule window.

"It is made up of the rings
of time. Each ring has its own character:
Natural Disasters—where whirlwinds and
firestorms clash—, Human and Animal History—
where all species of animals, extinct and
living, cluster in a large diffuse cloud—,
the band of Two Way Messages...."

And, in a glassy black quiet where the space
capsule floated freely, the ring of
True Stories.

Here, aparitions from the past, the present,
and the future gathered to meet the space
travellers.

About being born, slipping out of the womb
like a bead on a string, or like a railway car
with the others, brothers and sisters,
forepaws and backpaws,
ahead and behind.

Being born in a caul, coming feet first
so that your mother's teeth tear open
the membrane at the wrong end;

struggling to breathe as a knife, thin as a
razor, cuts the sac away from your nose
and your mouth.

(The hand holding the knife belongs to Mr.
Folchakov.)

A first cry. Eyelids sealed shut—pale blue
lids like the milkiest of seas.
Then your mother's tongue, like wet towels,
rubbing your body awake;
your lungs, weak balloons,
as they try to inflate.

Cold air, hard light,
and swimming away from these over the straw
to the shore of her body.

Blind eyes, blind mouth,
but your nose, like a compass, steering you
onto her breast.

Cold and death is a matter of inches.

"Welcome, Laika," said Mr. Folchakov,
long long ago.
"Welcome to the planet earth!"

Laika takes a drink from the specially
constructed container near her head, and she
and Mr. Folchakov gaze down at the dark spade-
like shadow on the earth that indicates the
Caucasus Mountains.
A few moments later,
Mr. Folchakov points out Mount Ararat,
and the two of them strain their eyes
for signs of Noah's ark.

Earth to Sputnik II, earth to Sputnik II...

◆

And so they passed further and further from the
diamond-shaped territory of the Western Soviet
Union.

◆

Laika looks from space to earth and back
again:

The curtain between us is not heat or light.
It is not skin.
The curtain is transparent, blue, colourless.

There is nothing beyond the curtain but space.
What you see when you look at the earth
is a rainbow.
The earth is not a prism.
It is a promise.

The eye is a prism. Mr. Folchakov has one
glass eye which he wears like a medal from the
last war.

Mr Folchakov was at Stalingrad. Mr.
Folchakov caught rats for large companies
of women and children starving in cellars.
Mr. Folchakov learned to cook.

Mr. Folchakov was the first Russian greeting
the first American to enter Berlin.
Mr. Folchakov drove a tank and kept chickens
inside it.
Mr. Folchakov took home six German toilet
bowls to his family in Gorky.
Mr. Folchakov stayed on his farm. He kept one
sheep and one calf alive. Mr. Folchakov
had a good war,

although he lost his family.

Mr. Folchakov was there when Laika was born.

What you see when you look at the earth
depends on your eyesight.
What Laika sees is the colour red. She views
seedlings inches below the soil,
the boiling sulphur waters of hot springs,
the steam of goats' urine as it strikes the
black rocks of the Caucasus Mountains;

the heat of a bird's heart as its shadow
crosses a salt lake.

Red heat radiates from the earth.
It makes a curtain that tears in the storm
in Laika's brain.

If only she could pull the curtain back
completely.
If only she could close her eyes and feel at
peace.
If only she could smell something more than
metal, and Mr. Folchakov,
and the heated rubber smell of scientific
instruments.
If only she could move her body away from
those tubes—one to feed her, one to empty.

It is not Mr. Folchakov's fault that the
capsule tumbles and tumbles.

Mr Folchakov looks from space to earth and
back again...

⟡

Calling all the world,
at eight o'clock today,
we were so far away,
and falling.

Riding through the stars,
the universe is ours,
locked in a metal world,
and falling.

Calling all the world,
to tell you where we've gone,
we're on our way beyond
your imagining.

Calling all the world,
we've gone so far away,
much further than we'd planned
we're travelling.

Calling all the world,
calling far from home,
we're out here all alone
and falling.

Sailing on a sea,
invisible but free,
in cold, in dark,
in beauty.

Calling all the world,
at eight o'clock today,
we were so far away,
and falling.

Calling. Calling
S.O.S. The Whole World.

✧

Mr Folchakov remembers peering through a
shoe-store fluoroscope:

everywhere he looks he sees bones surrounded
by green flesh. His bones were slightly
ridged, like tracks in sand; they were strung
together in links—he could see their
weaknesses.

So it is with the mountains: their ridges,
from a great height like this,
spray out from an axis like the limbs
of a skeleton.

This is not the whole story: the whole story
lies hidden in the earth: it is a monster
just now breaking surface.

The mountains are the hind parts of God.

Mr. Folchakov was at Stalingrad.
He killed a hundred Polish soldiers, who were
fighting for the Germans.
He saw his mother raped; he raped an innocent
child in Belgium.

Mr. Folchakov knows the hind parts of God
like the back of his hand.

There is a flickering light, like swamp gas
or the signal flares of paratroopers, outside
the spacecraft.

But there is no swamp, no vegetation, no
bodies falling through air while attached to
ropes.

There is only Folchakov and Laika, straining
to see what they cannot understand, tumbling
over and over, almost out of control,
squeezing the muscles of their stomachs tight
to fight the nausea

of a billion urgent questions breathing their
air.

❖

Earth to Sputnik II, earth to Sputnik II…

❖

This is a True Story.

At the Gasthof Sejkot, Luxenburgerstrasse,
Vienna, Mr. Sejkot sweeps snow from his
concrete steps. He goes back inside and
adjusts his toupée. Then he picks up the
newspaper which he had left on the bar, and
speaks to the plasterer who is tearing down a
wall in the dining room.

Mr. Sejkot reads: Illinois Housewife Receives Signal from Spacecraft: Every night when 32 year old Mary Shaker tries to sleep, she is kept awake by the satellite beep from Sputnik II. Somehow her metal bed frame is acting as a receiver. "The signal is three shorts and one long," said Mrs. Shaker. "Like Beethoven's Fifth Symphony."

He rattles his newspaper as he realises that
the plasterer isn't paying attention. "I am
telling you: this dog who is up in the sky,
this sputpup or pupnik or whatever you call
him—he is happy to be alive! He is happy, I
am saying, to be part of something important!"

✧

Outside, on the trees, there are ornaments of
crystal and pink glass.
Ladies in fur hats and coats, wearing
elegant boots and carrying pastries, stop to
look at them.

Ladies with blond hair and no hats cross the
street in front of traffic.
Horn-hooting is not allowed. But there is
music. *Du-du-du-dum. Du-du-du-dum,* sing the
irritated drivers.

Mr. Folchakov and Laika have been watching
this Story through the window of their
spacecraft.

They observe a woman in a fur hat and coat
and wearing elegant boots, sit down on the
front seat of a tram. She unpicks the
string from a cardboard box marked, "Aida."
She raises a nut-torte to her lips. Cream
sticks to her fingers, and she licks them one by one—
one, two, three, four, five—

as the tram passes a statue of Mozart,
as the tram passes Goethe sitting in snow
and follows the open carriage in which
Beethoven is catching his death of cold.

A little dog waits quietly within the
shelter of a tree bearing thin gold leaves.
Each leaf has been tied to a twig by a thin
gold thread. The dog's head pivots slowly
as it watches the tram go by. Six, seven,
eight, nine, ten...
the woman finishes licking her fingers...

...as Mr. Sejkot draws a cartoon of Marshall
Zukov on a corner of his newspaper...

...as Mr. Folchakov takes out a telescope to view Alexander the Great running alongside a train as it nears a border.

✧

"Ah…"

says Alexander, who has spotted Laika running beside him.

"It is the chow that jumped over the moon! That Russian sputpup isn't the first dog in the sky. That honour belongs to the dog star. But we're getting too *Sirius*. Ha. Ha. Ha!"

Mr. Folchakov, who is on the train holding out his hand to the running Alexander, now withdraws his help,
and Alexander is left
further and further behind. As is Laika.

"Mark my words!…"
shouts the Conqueror,

"When you Russians shoot cows into outer space, it will be the herd shot round the world!

"Moongrel! Mutnik! Pupnik! Woofnik! Every Dognik has its Daynik!…"

Mr. Folchakov firmly shuts the door to his compartment and settles back in his seat. Mr. Folchakov is going to cross this border alone.

Laika, in the spacecraft, shivers.

✧

I want to forget about where I am,

this metal raft,
these atmospheric waves,
this nothingness,

the shore of the earth bobbing like a cork
far below.

Tides sweep past the metal bowl in which I
am tethered.

I want to forget about where I am,

the pain that is my body,
the heat of the sun,
the cold black night,
the moon and planets, loosened from their
moorings,

which float like unconscious victims.

I want to forget about who I am,

this birth,
this whirling,
a beginning, a middle, an end.

I want to forget about where I'm going,
about what I am—

a story without a country,
without return.

Mr. Folchakov clears his throat. "Did they, uh, say anything to you about going back? I mean, do you know…?"

Laika turns her head away. Her heart
drums in her small chest. There is not
enough room for it and for what she is
feeling. Electrodes itch her skin. She
turns her head away away away.

Sunspots, like diamonds, blind her. Behind
them is the figure of a woman feeding a hot
furnace. A woman in a blue gown.

Laika with diamonds in her eyes. In her
ears. In her throat where they make small
cuts each time she swallows.
Laika dazzled out of her mind.

I won't think of anything, Laika thinks.
I'm going to be fine.
She does not feel Mr. Folchakov when he
touches her.
She does not feel his fear as—while riding in the
spacecapsule (still tumbling, tumbling)
—he finds himself on a train leaving
Alexander the Great far behind.

Mr. Folchakov does not see the woman at the
furnace.
He is nearing a border.
The train slows down.

Near the station there is a church and a
school.
There is an orphanage, a lying-in room, a
bronze monument to Alexander.

As the sky darkens with snow-clouds,
soldiers in uniform pour out of wooden sheds
and board the train.

The snow starts to blow.
Through the window of the train the border disappears.
Where there were fences and watchtowers, men patrolling with dogs,
are now dim shapes of snow and more snow.

A tall plump woman, wearing a black coat and headscarf,
tugs at the door to Mr. Folchakov's compartment.
The door is frozen shut. The ticket collector joins her.
They tug and tug.
Mr. Folchakov leaves the window and tries to assist.
All tug.

It is 4 degrees Centigrade inside the corridor.

The door cracks open.

The woman in the black coat picks up the pot of steaming Brockwurst which she had set down behind her.
Smiling, she lifts a sausage with a fork and offers it to Mr. Folchakov.
Smiling back, Folchakov accepts.
The sausage burns his fingers.

The woman frowns at the ticket-collector who reaches into his overcoat and pulls out a bottle of beer.
The woman takes it and gives it to Mr. Folchakov,
then she turns around and carries the pot down the corridor. She enters a cupboard in which there is a tiny fridge and a little stove on which another pot of Brockwurst boils.

A case of beer bottles and lemonade bottles
rests on the floor.

The woman returns to Mr. Folchakov bringing a
paper plate on which she has placed a dab of
mustard.

"Thank you," says Mr. Folchakov, smiling and
smiling. The woman smiles back. "Soon we will cross
the border," she says.

✧

Outside, the blizzard has lifted. A man with
no shirt on, and a man in a bear costume are
wrestling.
Passengers open their windows and throw out
money.

The soldiers leave the train.

Mr. Folchakov raises two fingers and sights
along them: crack crack—he pretends to fire
a rifle.
Near a watchtower a shadow stumbles and falls.
Crack, crack, crack.

The woman is standing just behind Folchakov.
"Now you are part of the land," she says.

✧

Over the fields, pack jogging on his back,
spectacles fogged with rain,
Mr. Folchakov runs toward a Red Cross hut.

It is the same field of frozen cabbages that
his grandfather crossed in 1917. The red roof
is still ruined; ivy winds round the fire-
blackened posts.

It is the same place exactly. Mr. Folchakov,
dressed in a greatcoat and wearing fingerless
gloves,
runs toward a secret destination.

Somewhere he has left behind a child.
Somewhere soldiers stuff festive branches into
the muzzles of their guns.

Police examine the view all the way to the
river.
He has got to keep moving.

Somewhere else, there is blue sky,
white stones, and a beach on which waves crash
loud as machine guns.
Policemen and soldiers patrol the border.
Their boots crush stones to gravel.
Somewhere, down narrow streets, the smell of
fresh bread floods up to the windows.

Mr. Folchakov blinks. He remembers a pen
where sheep were slaughtered. He remembers a
horse, nickering for bread, rolling over and
over, down the lip of a valley.

He sees a jeep drive up to a shadow. Soldiers
get out and unsling their rifles. "Get a move
on!" shouts their leader.

Soldiers lift the body. "Get a move on! Just
drive!"

Yes, yes indeed, Mr. Folchakov has crossed the
border.

Meanwhile, back in the spacecapsule, the
clouds over Europe have receded.
Mr. Folchakov snores quietly. His train,

snaking across the countryside far far below,
continues on its way.

Laika is listening to music: *Du-du-du-dum.
Du-du-du-dum.*

In their seats, at a concert, children hold
bells in their laps.
Laika listens intently, her ears pricking, as
at the conductor's signal, and only then, the
children ring their bells.

Ring, ring. With a flash of his palm the
conductor signs them to stop.

The music pours on, like cream over snow.

A white horse is pulling a sleigh at a
spanking pace across the snowy steppe. A
watchful dog sits wrapped up warm next to the
driver. A dog that barks in response to the
sleigh bells, the snapping of icicles from
branches, the cushion of snow everywhere that,
despite the cold, makes her feel safe.

Laika feels a warm hand on her cold nose,
and opens her eyes to look into the deep
understanding eyes of Mr. Folchakov.

There, there, the eyes say, I understand.
As the stars break up all around them. Like
thin ice.
Like a wrenched mirror.

✧

Earth to Sputnik II. Earth to Sputnik II.

✧

"The capsule!"
shouts Mr. Folchakov.
"It's stopped tumbling!"

They are on a smooth deep stream the indigo
blue colour of old bottle glass....
They are being towed to the moon
by a team of wild swans....

Laika closes her eyes, and like a newborn,
makes little sucking movements. She nestles in
close to the chest of Mr. Folchakov. She
likes being here on the stream of glass. She
likes smooth sailing.

She has forgotten where she is.
Certainly she has forgotten the tubes of
oxygen, the emptying cylinders, the lowering
level of water in the special container.
She has even forgotten her hunger.

A bell rings. It is time to eat. But Laika
doesn't hear.

Mr. Folchakov hears. But he is panting with
the effort of struggling through deep snow
in wet boots.
He has arrived at the Berlin Wall.

He reaches out to touch it.
It stretches as far as he can see across his
path.

But where are the cars, the people?

He begins to climb. Shots ring out,
and he watches a shadow, like a shell peeled
from its core,
fall into deep snow.

It chars its way into the earth...
while a ring of black-coated soldiers
gather around it.

Laika rests, panting. She hears the soft
rattle in Mr. Folchakov's throat.
She would like him to wake up. She wants it
to be Christmas, Easter, May Day.
She wishes to see a parade of children,
dressed in identical red and gold uniforms,
manoeuvering hoops. She would like to wear
a ruff around her neck, and perch on a
horse's saddle in front of a beautiful lady.
She would like

not to be where she is.

The blue sea below.
And nearby. Nearest. A lady in a blue
dress tending a furnace.

*"The great spaceship shuddered briefly as it
went into hyperdrive and headed for the
Whirlpool Galaxy. Captain Dart watched the
hand of the C-meter. It was close to the
speed of light, and getting closer and
closer. He felt no change, of course, but he
knew that his personal time was already
running slow. Each tick of the clock,
each heartbeat took months or years of earth
time. How old were his friends on earth? he
wondered. How long had they been dead?"*

Laika looks down and sees a mushroom-shaped
cloud puff up from the centre of the ocean.

The cold blue sea is covered with voyagers
moving in circles.

The currents carry them swiftly towards the
unknown.
Laika is swimming, swimming, swimming,
looking for someone to rescue.
And, of course, looking for land.

The Daily Mirror:
"The dog will die and we can't save it!"

We of the League Against Cruel Sports, feel
nothing but horror and contempt for the
behavior of the Russian scientists, besides
which the sickening stories of the inhuman
cruelties of the Middle Ages fade into
insignificance…

Dr. Pietor Pokrovsky, Soviet physiologist,
said at a Moscow press conference that no
means of returning Laika to earth had been
included in the satellite because the
Russians had "not yet fully solved" the
problem of recovering satellite contents.

Laika takes a sip of water. Mr. Folchakov
wipes his brow with his handkerchief.

(We are the stars. We turn through the bowl
of the sky.
We touch its rim and sing a thousand notes.

We are the stars. The cold and lonely
hours. As on a quiet road at night,
we take our place in the landscape.)

A streak of gorgeous light—white, blue,
yellow, red—rushes through the earth's
atmosphere.

"Oh!…"
says Mr. Folchakov who is now wide awake….
"Look, Laika, look who has come!"

Just outside of the capsule, keeping up with
them by taking rapid strides, is the composer
Prokofiev! His bald head and his spectacles
reflect the colours of the meteors which
continue to fall, and which form an escort to
the falling spacecraft.
Prokofiev calls out to them:

"There is, I believe, a certain similarity
with shooting at moving targets—only by
taking aim ahead of the moving objects, of
taking aim at "Tomorrow" so to speak, will
you not remain behind, remain with the
demands of yesterday."

We journey west.
We follow sun and moon.
Ocean leads to land to ocean.
There is just one circle,
this earth we know.

Laika and Folchakov wave goodbye to
Prokofiev. They wave at the woman in blue.
They dip their paddles into the thick black
lake of space.

Far, far over the ocean of black sky, past
islands in uncharted waters...

*Earth to Sputnik II... Earth to Sputnik II...
Cosmonaut, answer. Answer....*

Folchakov and Laika look at each other.
Mr Folchakov rubs his hand underneath his
shirt collar.

"It is very hot!"

Calling all the world,
at eight o'clock today,
we were so far away,
and falling.

Riding through the stars,
the universe is ours,
locked in a metal world,
and falling.

Calling all the world,
to tell you where we've gone,
we're on our way beyond
your imagining.

Calling. Calling.
S.O.S. The Whole World.

LOVE AS IT IS

Love above all, don't you agree?
Love above all when one's star
is in the ascendent, art above all
when the star is in decline.
Listen to the voice that sings love
and not to the voice that explains it.

— *George Sand*
(Aurore Dudevant)

Antiquities

I Have Been Dreaming About the Wife

I have been dreaming about the wife
of a newly dead man. I have heard the air

thicken with news, and voices saying to her,
Christine, you are wearing a red sweater.

That the dead notice such things,
or that we think the dead miss us so

they are compelled to say,
Do not wonder where I am,

I am here, with you!

I have seen a man touch a woman
only so that he, himself, will not disappear.

I have watched the wife of the newly dead man
buy a waterfall of colour to wear.

Christine, I like the pink stockings,
Christine, I like the way you wear your hair.

No, don't change anything,
stay how you were.

In the dream no one is beautiful,
the dead man does not appear,

only his wife, and the voices saying:
Christine, you are familiar.

Being True

I am in prison.
Now you cannot find me.
I make a prison in the dark with my body.
I make this prison so I will not escape you.

Dance with me. On this small concrete floor,
let your bare feet feel the cold.
The keys are here,
under my pillow.

Dance out of the dark and away.

Unlock these handcuffs
so that I may touch you.
What happens when the four walls break?

Visiting hour. We have nothing to say.
Let us use our lips to kiss.
I know how to love. It will come back.

I want you to go.
I want you to find me in this dark
and pull me out.

Let us meet somewhere else.

If I do not dream,
if I have no dreams to betray me.

The Red Factory
for Herbert Dacker

Near where I lived,
where the alcohol factories were,

the sound from them was always there,

and the door to the stairway open

with strange men in it;

and clouds at night
yellow with streetlight.

Rain ran down the cobblestones
to the bottom of the hill

where the smokestacks grew,

and women were espaliered on walls,
torn dresses scattered:

the children went home at dawn
to fall from windows.

Near where I lived,
wildflowers bloomed between the stones,

long grass threaded whitely
up to the lintels—

there was broken glass, milk cartons,
a dead kitten.

We gave our toys away before they vanished.

Bronze statues with eyes that looked through you,
bone enameled under the skin,
rain-washed in the open—

the industry went on all the time,
sending up clouds of steam—

a hundred faces giving last looks.

Christmas in Prague, 1986

The grey smoke of the trees behind the slow snowfall,
the grey walls of the city, like empty bank vaults;

such delicate things are spirits, yet they flicker behind the
snow, the curtain of trees, over the closed

doors and windows; they touch the changeless faces of the
people.
In the gold-makers' land, a man sets up a stall.

In his art, Christ and the Virgin sleep,
three shepherds kneel in adoration—red, yellow, blue—

against the pale horizon. They have no money, but they
look and remember.

The crowds press near, their pockets are empty:
see how they take the snow in their hands to warm it.

An old man steps from the curtain of trees—
his red cloak, his wild hair, blow in the wind.

Soon he is running, his song spills over the snow,
it changes to gold.

What music is this that sets the thousand bells
of the city ringing? What gold coins are these

that chime on the ice in his footsteps?
The people stand, frozen, as the fingers of spirits

press at their throats; as the wild birds of spring

beat their wings in the splintered air;
as their faces blur with weeping.

Native Land

Three or four farms left now, plus a dog and Mme Hélène,
where on Christmas Eve, 1944, thirty-two young men

were shot by the Germans;

and the forest where one man ran, crossing the road,
jumping a stream.

Fog freezes to the branches—
the dead appear

like sea anemones behind shop windows.

Their village has fallen,
their guards are weeping. White-faced as metal

they exhibit belongings: pocket watches, a helmet,
self-portraits.

Even the stones are clock-marked with bullets.

Love, we stand in a grove of birches, we pull our coats tight
against the wind. Bullets fly backwards

into the mouths of our guns.

This is the picture to step in:
now we are part of the land.

My Dear Friends

In the hotel room, a piece of paper has shifted;
there is the smell of sweat. Those were not our hands
opening drawers. Nor are these our soldiers,
dressed in black, searching beneath the train.

A man on hands and knees examines the corridors,
an old woman on a tram takes your arm.
How to explain this?—she wants you to stay;

you must not leave them in this lost city.

My dear friends, someone kneels on the tracks
ahead of you—still will you go?

This city, with its black towers,
is streets where our bodies, like pale
splintered wood, drift—

look at the hillside: in the sun's gold *there*
you see our blood.

These bent heads, these shoes fragile as paper,
the fresh snow, the terrible angels in churches:

we will wait for you. We have come to watch you go.

For the last time we touch hands. Slowly the train
leaves the empty station. When we look back,

it is you who have turned to stone.

Let us drink to the children conceived this summer,
let us touch hands once more.

Let us show you the city that never fell,
the empty city,
where people kneel on the land
and dig under the ashes.

Please, let us show you.

We do not feel the cold.
Our children walk naked on ice.
They lie hidden beneath the trains.

When the soldiers come,
it means nothing.

Prague-Köln-Berlin

Madrigal,
a Lullaby for Xan

She sleeps, her dreams as clear as diamond edge
that cuts the icy sky in black and white,
the stars are palest candles to her light.

The dark spills over sill and window ledge,
a river foaming bleakly through the night.
She sleeps, her dreams as clear as diamond edge
that cuts the icy sky in black and white.

The wren that sings its heart-song through the sedge,
and braves the hunter hawk in its full flight,
dreams of its mate and nest soon in its sight:
she sleeps, her dreams as clear as diamond edge
that cuts the icy sky in black and white,
the stars are palest candles to her light.

Letter from Portugal

Like beautiful bodies of the dead who had not grown old
and they shut them, with tears, in a magnificent mausoleum,
with roses at the head and jasmine at the feet—
this is how desires look that have passed....
                              (from "Desires" by Cavafy)

I always begin my letters to you with a kiss,
and so you probably think I frequently dream.
Our room has dark turquoise walls
like the sea far below the white chalk cliffs.
The children are sleeping in the alcove,
short, difficult breaths they hold;
I can hear the restaurant down below,
I can hear the knives.
I am speaking to you about my dream of cold,
like beautiful bodies of the dead who had not grown old.

I found a folded map beneath the bed,
I am speaking about the dream of you I had,

and a ship's name printed in gold.
I am reminding you of how our hands touched,
and that it was as though we'd planned it—
blowing out the candles of our love without a reason,
as we parted from each other in a flurry of desperate
leavetakings;
the chance for happiness was not worth risking:
lovers and desires, they only last a season:
they shut them, with tears, in a magnificent mausoleum.

What do you think? It doesn't matter much,
for we live, after all in our hearts.
I shall leave you with a list,
small, perfect as an orchid's eye, as precious:
there are white dog roses on the cliffs,
and geraniums like flames blooming in the heat,
and much to learn from the tide's turning—
navigation by the stars, map-making,
astrolabe and sextant, the use of charts, all neat,
with roses at the head and jasmine at the feet.

Is it the death of love, everywhere, that I'm seeing?
There's a warm breeze, the blown sand stings my skin alive to feeling,
I am at the end of the world (a place called Sagres),
we look across to Cabo Saint Vincent through a haze of flowers,
orange tiled roofs, white-washed walls, the wind rising.
Navigators leave, with visions glorious and vast—
they are blinded by the sun, they lose their reason—
decaying anchors sleep on the shore, the leavers' leavings—
I see everything as if in a photograph with double cast:
this is how desires look that have passed.

Tranquille

I return to the bees,
to the cloud of them that razored the air
above the path to Roxana's house,

their white hives in two rows
like a landing field below—

they were swaying, like a giant bell
on an invisible dancer,

or as if the Mediterranean sea curled
and lipped at them.

Your bees, King Gargoris, colonizing
to the furthest reaches of the west,

the cold Pacific.

I had left you by then.
The liquidizing melt

of skin on skin,

the slow casting glances
from sky to river as we turned

were adrift like messages
in bottles. I could not track them,

had no idea where or when
they would turn up.

Until this,
the great bee kingdom.

I ached to dance the ringing bee dance,
strip clean

and clasp the cutting bees around my wrists
for bracelets.

I ached for honey, pain, and you.

The bees, in swarm, moved off.
Roxana, trailing golden nets,

came to gather them.

She, like some priestess
of that far off time

was veiled, slow and sure

as the sky, the sea,
the moon, the unharmed world.

I felt the golden kernel
kick to life inside.

I turned to run,
could smell the pines,

the heat, the blood that ran
when I refused to yield to you,

and sensed, again, the growing
child within the knives:

the myths are all of him,
I do not figure.

Roxana, carrying bees, murmurs,
Tranquille. Tranquille.

Flowers

What are these flowers
that I pull from my fingers,
their roots in my veins,

their colour and fluid
my breath and bone?

Sweet flowers that need no tending.
My arms ache with the weight of them,

the violet and pansy,
which sprang from the blood of Attis
as he maimed himself, and smelled the sweet scent
of the pine.

But there is no blood here.

I spread my hands like fans on the pale sheets
and behold the flowers while you are quiet, sleeping.

I touch your cheek. My fingers leave a print.

You turn, stirring the flowers, the pines,
the white bedcover, the sea I was born in.

Antiquities,

we lie on the soft bank of the river,
flies walk the sharp trajectories

of shoulder blades
and hips.

In the centre of the pelvic bones
are discs—

two golden suns engraved with antelope.
The surprise is steel,

the tip of a spade
that chinks,

and the hand within a glove
that tries my rings.

I was blind,
I felt the history of your tongue

for one last on my eyes:
I would have spoken,

I would have cried our love aloud,
but they broke us

like pottery or glass,
anything else that doesn't last.

The Mercers

The House at Mercer's Cove

Tomorrow is Sunday.
I go to the kitchen to peel the vegetables.

I gather up my sewing.

In the morning we have breakfast—salt fish
from the storehouse.

At lunch we wash the dishes.

We read the Bible, sing some hymns,
have supper,

then lay the large white cloth
over the table.

Unnecessary work can wait till Monday.

I forgot to say that the house has small framed windows.
It is made of wood, and freshly painted for winter.

Where could I go? To Lizzie's?
Aunt Prudence up the hill?

The girls from here work as maids in Montreal.

In the Front Room

is an organ.
I look past it to the ocean.

My sister's husband's son
disappeared from a boat,

my sister's husband's sister
went away down south:

she never came back,
dead, we think,

in a train wreck.

Three bedrooms, a dining room and living room,
the back kitchen:

I can drive the sleigh when I want
to Coley's Point.

Partridge berries after the first hard frost,
hot bakeapple drink for the children,

you'd give the mummers a bit of cake and a glass of clingy
when they'd come.

No drinking.
No dancing (except, perhaps, for the R.C.'s).
No playing cards.

Lamb cooked for dinner on Good Friday,
and herring.

I comb my hair.
I put on a dress and collar.

I dance in my room.
I try on rings.

My fingers make no sound.

I look past the cliff to Coley's Point
where the birds whirl round.

I see the split in the sky
where the angels fly.

I see the break in the sea
where the boats dance, helplessly.

I take off my rings.
I look out at the sky, the sea, the road,
the truth.

When the Men are Gone to Sea

we do the garden. We cut the hay, spread it to dry,
and rake it into a pook.

We have the garden, and the hens and the haying.

I sit at night by the open door and tear up rags.
Blue for my eyes (and his!),
brown for my hair,
red, yellow, green, orange,
the colours of the hills.

You never see a man up here in summer:
they're all gone down to Labrador.

If you see one you wonder,
knit stockings for winter

(blue,
brown).

I Lie Down

on the ice on the bay.
The stars swim slowly by.

This is the pain the men feel when they drown,
this is why they won't swim.

Men and women, a linked chain
crossing the ocean from Jersey Island.

This is all I know of my family.

The ice shapes itself to my body.
I feel tongues of ice on my bones.

I make a list of the vegetables
we put in the cellar:
cabbage, carrots, onions, beets and turnips.

We've a pig to kill for Christmas.

I've made a doll with blueberries for eyes,
for Zelah.

Black currant, gooseberries, wild raspberries
on low bushes.

Still the cold plays its scales of music.

Apple trees. Cherry trees.
These are like dreams,

heat-soaked,
sweet, saltless.

I lick the tears that freeze at my nostrils.

My father would laugh if he saw me like this,
then whip me.

I Touched the Swelling

on the child's wrist
and felt the knob of pain.

I held that flower
and gently breathed away its petals.

I could put my hand on a red-hot stove and not be burned.
I could wake up hungry
and find bread in the fields.

A storm blows in.

I pull down the blinds, and throw the kitchen mats
across the stove to spare us lightning.

Here is what we owed once Gosse took most of the fish
at the end of the season:

money to pay the doctor, the church, the school.

The Black Horse

is gone.
I've walked the fifteen miles to get her
more than once.

I sent Dorcas to borrow some books from Prudence.
"Tell your sister she's read all the books we've got.
Tell her to read her Bible," she said.

The R.C.'s draw their blinds.
King Billy's flags fly over the road.

Rock, meadow, the sea,
this is my world.

The men belong to the Orange Lodge.

One Heater to Heat the Whole House

Once you went to bed in those feather mattresses,
you couldn't move.

Everyone had gardens.
Now they've all gone to the commons.

Father's Bible in four volumes....

My love. So much to do before bad weather sets in.

And you gone long before, stepping off along the shoreline,
land for your children.

Eight Poems for Margaret
July-August, 1989

The packers are done.
The three-quarter moon slips through the sky
in slow time.

You lie in the bath.
Your tennis shorts—a gift to me—
blow on the line.

The house is quiet,
all the things you loved in it, gone.

The garden was all your care:
nasturtium, rose, chrysanthemum,
cat mint—

the two black cats
from next door,
roll in it—

black-eyed susan, and sweet pea,
gentians, alyssum;

the bird house filled with bread;

roses that colour the spaces between
the spin-around clothes line

where your tennis shorts swing.

Pink clouds colour the city
where Margaret once ran,

her steps bright as water in sunshine.

Now you lift a thin thigh from the bath—
tomorrow we're going.

You had prizes at school for needlepoint and singing...

the open mouths of the livingston daisies,
closing.

She dreams of falling,
but it is not she who slips
through the rails,

it is the white figure of a girl,
or the ghost of a girl,
who has never lived.

Margaret is too substantial to fall
or to be pushed:
it is unimaginable.

I put on her old tennis shorts,
fresh from the line,

and go out in the garden.
Dry soil breaks in my hands.

She said here, plant the roses here,
they will not fail.

A white butterfly
flips past the window,

over the stair-rail
and down, I presume,

into the garden.
What a garden it is!

Twenty wasp stings for the poor man
building our fence—

we have found him a bee-hat since—

wood left over from building,
and pink tufts of insulation

flapping, like sea-wrack.

Underneath it all, Margaret,
as you can see,

are the ferns and moss, and bluish-white Indian pipe

so ghostly a hue;

and the gooseberries—
the canes almost hidden, bent by the weight
of the fruit:

they lie on the earth
and are heaped with pine-needles,

trash, leaves, dog feces, compost.
We have plans for this place:

with you I've mapped a rose-garden
where the warped and windy shed stands.

The cats will forgive us tearing it down,
though they haunt it now

as if there were no other refuge.

Refuge, why that word now,
when I am helpless to help you?

The moon rose upside down
in Africa, you say.

A good day. The drugs mute the pain,

you forget why.

You iron a few shirts, grow tired,
watch golf on television,

have tea with friends.
The day, for me, drones on.

I fix photographs into an album,
finish the ironing.

Ask God again how could he be so
wrong.

There is thunder this evening,
the dog cowers in the kitchen.

I lean on the stove, uselessly weeping.

✧

My bed is my island,
my refuge.

But what is a bed to you
in the night hours

that toll
to the treble of your radio?

Even in my grief
I can turn across the swell

and find love,
mute now in its terror for you,

but there, afloat.

What comforts you?
Just the radio.

You lie in a hospital bed at home.
You will not let me raise it up
to ease you.

It is only a bed, your stubbornness tells me.

You wrap your hair in curlers.
I do not know what gives you the strength
to do it.

Oh plain death. You have no mirror.

I turn in bed to touch my husband's hand.

Not in my house,
she won't die here, we won't let her,
he says.

We hear thunder,
and brace ourselves.

✧

I sit up in bed and say it aloud—
Hope.

In the morning we consult the bird book,
arguing over robins *here* and *there.*
Ours are bigger, a kind of thrush.
Margaret's are small, bright feathered,
birds she's known all her life.

Who's right?

I mop and dust and vacuum.
The baby cleans and polishes all the stones.

Good-morning. I am a spirit in search of
wind, snow, sun.
I am a soul marooned in ice;
I am swimming the band of water
that swims the earth,
the universe,

the chorus of spirits.

I am holding my breath and travelling through this unknown
sea without a mask.

The wind shakes the trees,
salty and sweet.

Margaret sits in a deck chair,
sleeping.

Say a word to her and she is, at once,
awake.

But she is tapping her way, eyes closed,
into another landscape.

The new fence is almost finished,
the dogs roam its edges

and pee on it.
What is the word for 'escape'?

Margaret knows it.

She sits up to ask if a debt has been paid,
to say she is too much trouble,

to speak of her son's young friend,
years ago.

"He's in jail now," she says sadly.
She cannot get up.

Yesterday we lost the key to the medicine box.
Had the baby hidden it,

or was this a way to tell us, 'enough is enough'?
What line is being crossed

as she shifts her thin legs
on the chair slats?

She says she smells roses—
fine gardener that she is,

the labour and pleasure of those years
follow her.

We sort herbs into jars:
they are musky and tepid in odour.

Roses, she says, roses. The sweetness
makes her smile. The scent that pursued the saints

billows about her.

❖

Now is the time
for rejoicing at her life,

at the wind that quarters the trees,
and the sun and cool morning.

As when the 1st battalion
of the West African Frontier Regiment

played, for her, the Hausa Farewell
as she left Nigeria,

so now there is a salute to be given.

Let the wind give it,
and the trees,

and the light beyond this room.

Let her be stepping now,
as she walked, in 1948,

up the airplane steps,
boldly under the sun,

while the band played.

*Blow far winds blow,
the east cold.*

Margaret has gathered her gifts about her,

she walks the white stones.

A Cold Departure:
The Liaison of George Sand and
Frederyk Chopin

George Sand's Letter
George Sand to Wojciech Grzymala in Paris
Nohant, June 1838

It would never occur to me to doubt your sincerity.
Let us state the question clearly:
one must put one's own happiness last
when the happiness of those we love
claims all our strength.

I looked at the sun—
a yellow pinhole
with blackness all around it.

I looked at the skeleton
inside my hands:

the fingers danced
like black burnt sticks.
I looked at my heart:
it curled at the edges,

its juice spilled
into the cavity
of my body.

I put my hands in there:
the little black sticks stirred—

there was nothing there
for you.

I moved my knees,

I lifted my feet
and danced in the colour yellow.

I made claw-marks in the earth:
I scratched its lens.

I made a wound
and watered it from the heart.
I carried it in my hands

and brought it to you.

Is this what is meant by love,
by happiness?

Give me a clear, straightforward and categorical answer.
Is she the right one to secure his happiness?
I am not asking whether he loves her.
What I want to know is which of the two of us he must
give up. His nature seems too unstable
to stand great anguish.

I will not battle with his childhood friend.
We did not deceive each other. All the same,
we had to come back to earth
when the divine flame had cooled.
The song of angels beckons us heavenwards.
For myself I refuse to give way to passion.
Heaven is where we meet. So my duty is fully mapped.

But I can, without forswearing myself,
perform it two distinct ways.
I could slip into his thoughts.
I could from time to time permit a chaste embrace.
I could keep as far as possible away [from Chopin].

The man is on the bed.
I lie next to him.

This boat steers itself.
I think we will drown.

Sea-beasts rise from the floor:
I cannot remember more.
I promise you

they were not of this world.

Which of the two of us,
who surrenders?

It is an easy birth,

but I have no recollection
of having done it.

The man on the bed—
as I rolled away from his body,
as I drew a circle of prayer—

there was a waterfall of colour.

So I shut my eyes
and swam.

*Marriage or any similar union would be the graveyard
of his artist soul. Happiness
as a family man is out of the question.
It will be for you to tell me if I am wrong.*

*I am convinced one is a better human being
when one loves with sublime emotion.
One rather draws near to God.*

*I have no wish to steal anyone from anyone—
I have too much respect for the notion of property—
unless it be prisoners from their gaolers,
victims from their executioners,
Poland from Russia.*

Nothing is so precious as a fatherland,
and a man who has one already must not make unto himself
a new one.

And the Lord said unto me, Give,
and I held out my hand.

And the Lord said unto me, Give,
and I held out my other hand.

And he said again, Give.
I looked at the trees that were bending.
I said, Lord, I would do anything.

He said, Give.

I said, Lord I have had visions and dreams.

He said, Give.

I began to weep. He said, Give.
I began to sing:

and dreamt that I swam naked at midnight,
and dreamt that I swam away from my husband,
and dreamt that I hid from my children under a stone.

A white stone. Then a black stone.
I dreamt that the Lord kept moving the stones.

And the Lord said, Give.

Consumed am I by thy fire.
By the fire of the pit.
The cypress trees are wilted, scorched, burnt up.

The Lord said, Give.

White foamy milk poured from my breasts.

My child cried and cried.

I would do anything, Lord, I said.

Everyone is born like a stone slipping
down inside a dress.
A smooth stone

that falls quickly.

A mother bends and picks it up.
She warms it in her hand.

Years later, turning out the pockets
of an old coat, she finds it.

Tears come to her eyes.

Everyone who is born is in pain.
Everyone is fearful of strangers.

He said, Give.

Here is my body, Lord.
It melts like wax. It is a candle in the earth.

He said, Give, give, give.

I shall represent for him an Italy
which one visits and enjoys on spring days
but where one cannot remain permanently,
because there is more sunshine than beds and tables.

Poor Italy! A land that one dreams of,
longs for or regrets;
but where no one can remain, since she herself is unhappy
and cannot impart a happiness she does not possess.

On a train travelling
through the mountains of Italy:
lake after lake, white-cliffed,
fathomless,
inviting.

A villa on a hillside,
a trip down into town:

at Como the lake
licks the city walls.

We play house in the villa:
floors and tables,
cutting boards,

a gecko in a marble drawer
with dusty cutlery.

At night bonfires prick the shore.

One white sheet on the balcony.
Brought in.

*There is one last supposition that it is right
for me to mention. It may be that he no longer loves
this childhood friend at all.
My good friend, be his guardian angel.
You must save him from the too relentless claims
of conscience, save him from his own virtue.*

*Whoever, in return for a certain
finite amount of devotion, calls for the devotion
of another's whole future life
is asking something wicked.*

*I loathe seducers. A vow of love and faithfulness
is crime and cowardice when the lips utter
what the heart disavows.*

We shall not see each other every day;
every day we shall not be consumed by the sacred fire,
but there will be some fine days and some holy flames.

The dance you dance
is east to west:

each step of the dance
is a wish.

The dance you dance now
is the dance of naming women.

I give up my name.
I give up my dancing feet.
I give up my spirit.

A green meadow on the sea,
a house with seven rooms to think in:

keep him safe,
keep him with me.

I sit and overcome my pain.

My heart is an agony. For you are there
and I touch you here,

here.

I have sometimes been mistaken about people
but never about myself. My feelings have always
been stronger than my rational thinking,
and the boundaries I have tried to fix for myself
have proved useless.

I have changed my ideas a score of times.
Above all I have believed in faithfulness.
Others have failed me and I have failed them;
yet I felt no remorse.

Whenever I was unfaithful I was the victim
of a kind of fatality,
of my own instinctive urge towards the ideal,
which compelled me to leave what was imperfect
for something which seemed closer to perfection.

What did we think we could do for each other?
Enter a mirror?

What looks back through the glass
is a spirit trying to enter itself.

Everything inside the mirror is dead.

This is my gift:
I stepped inside.

I have loved as an artist, as a woman, a sister, a mother,
a nun, a poet. Some of these loves have been born
and have died in a single day.
Some have driven me to despair,
others have kept me cloistered in a state
of extreme spirituality.

And all the time I have been perfectly sincere.

My whole nature moved into these different phases.
I have appeared what I truly am:
one who revels in all that is beautiful,
who is hungry for the truth, sensitive in her feelings,
weak in her judgments, often ridiculous, always sincere,
never petty or vindictive,
not inclined to suffer fools gladly and, thank God,
quick to forget evil things and evil people.

I stood at the door of the clinic.
I carried my baby in my arms.

I put a stone on the table.
I said, Here, doctor, eat my bread.

I put white stars on the table.
I said, Here, doctor, eat my fire.

I put the torn fabric of the sky
on the table.
I said, Here, doctor, cover the dead
with this.

I put the baby on the table.
I dressed her in stones and fire.
I dressed her in rags.
I married her to the dead.

I said, Here, doctor, set me on fire.
I put a match on the table.

I said, Here, doctor, build me a house.
I put smoke on the table.

I said, Here, doctor, cut me with this.
I put my hands on the table.

I lifted up my child.
She had bread, a wedding dress,
she had a house roofed with blood.

I said, Here, doctor, take my life.
I said, Here, doctor, breathe the baby alive.

He said, No.
I am too tired.
He said, No.

I put my knife on the table.
I opened my mouth.
The table drowned in blood.

He said, No.

There my dear friend, you have my life.
You see it is nothing to boast of.
There is nothing to admire, much to be pitied,
nothing which a kind heart will condemn.

I am certain that those who accuse me
of having been an evil woman have lied,
and I could easily prove it if I took the trouble
to draw on my memories and tell my story:

but I have not the patience to do it,
and my memories are as short-lived as my rancours.

I can taste the baby.
The shock of her pain.

I can taste her blindness.

I can taste the baby—
her life runs away
like liquid,

her life dances like infant birds
aroused by a scream.

Her life curls and uncurls
against my dead thighs.

I can taste the baby
at the moment you leave me.

You have my life:
put it in human shape.

You have my life:
find it.

You have my life:
I hear it crying, abandoned
in a Spanish *caverna*.

My mouth touches your mouth,
and I taste the lives of infants.

This is my baby, my baby.

I lose her.

❖

I have never deceived anyone
and have never ceased to be faithful
unless I had very strong reasons which
through another's fault, had killed my love.

I am not of an inconstant nature. On the contrary,
I am so used to giving my exclusive affection
to one who loves me truly, so slow to take fire,
so accustomed to living with men without reflecting
that I am a woman,

that I was rather disturbed and frightened at the effect
this little person [Chopin] had on me.

I still have not got over my amazement.
It was a case of a sudden invasion
and it is not in my nature to regulate my conduct
by reason when love takes command.

So I am not blaming myself;
but I can plainly see that I am still very susceptible
and frailer than I thought I was.

Sleep descends on me
like a dove.

Its metal cry
is in my ears.

I swallow it whole,
where it is imprisoned.

Living creatures, letters,
music,

the children you cannot have—
I open myself to these,

and we dance, we two,
me and you.

Your thought is my thought.
In this secret place

we dance with elegance.
All the tortures are ours,
and the pleasures.

A tree clicks its dry leaves.

I look up at the apples,
I close my eyes

while light falls through the open window
of the sky above.

They want us to go on
although we have given up:

the gods who don't exist,
who refuse to accept us.

✧

What does it matter? It saddens me.
I shall have to tell lies like the rest of them.
That, I can assure you, is more mortifying
to my good opinion of myself
than to be mocked for a bad novel
or hissed for a bad play.

I should have kept a better watch over my eyes
and ears, above all my heart.

But if Heaven would have us remain faithful
to earthly affections, why does it sometimes
allow angels to lose their way among us
and meet us in our paths?

I love you,
but still you doubt.

We are changed in the light of that fact.
Touch.

Your hand splits the shadow
from the lamp.

You open the window.

I am the shadow.
You are the dance.

You are gone.
The cup of tea cools;
leaves stir in the corner

beneath the open window:

*And so the great question of love
arises once more within me.*

What shall I do with it?

I turn it over.
I prick it with a needle:

it leaks a clear liquid.
it could be tears.

*When one has allowed one's soul to be invaded,
when one has granted the simplest caress,
urged to it by the feeling of love,
the infidelity has already been committed.*

*What follows is less serious,
for he who has lost the heart has lost everything.*

*Hence, as a matter of principle,
I think that a total consecration of the new bond
does little to aggravate the initial fault,
but rather that the attachment may become more human
more powerful and dominating after possession.*

That is quite probable, and even certain.

*And so, when two persons wish to live together,
they should not violate nature and truth
by retreating from a complete union.*

*If he had asked for it in Paris
I should have yielded.*

All winter I have watched the light fade,

all spring I have waited for your hand
to lift me above the round world

like the moon,

like the womb that dreamed me,

like the spin
of a foreign sea.

You love my daughter.
We love you.

You love my son—
take everything you want—

my memories will begin
with you.

I hear my father.
The horse stops at the scene
of his accident—

I get off
and listen for death.

The trees are my music.

I have no tongue,
it is here, on paper.

I have no body,
it is counting money.

Soon someone must come
to save us.

✧

It will cost me dear to see our angel [Chopin] suffer.
I am not a child. I could well observe
that his human passion was making rapid strides
and that it was time we kept apart.

*That is why, the night before I left, I did not wish
to be left alone with him and I practically turned you both
out of doors.*

*And since I am telling you everything,
I wish to say that he displeased me by one single thing—
the fact that he had had in his own mind the wrong reason
for abstaining.
Until that moment I had considered it a fine thing
that he abstained out of respect for me, out of shyness,
even out of fidelity to another.
It was that which charmed and allured me the most in him.
But just as he was leaving, as if to overcome a final
temptation, he said two or three words
which did not at all correspond to my ideas.*

*He seemed to despise the coarser side of human nature,
and to fear to soil our love by further ecstasy.
I have always loathed this way of looking
at the final embrace of love.*

These stones that we lay on the path,
the white shells that spell
your name,

the violets
dusted with sand—

these are permanent.

Not the wickedness,
not the evil thought

that entered your brain,
not the dish that shattered.

I wanted to kill you—
but is that our love?

We cut an orange,
we share;

there are guests, invited
and uninvited:

is that our love?

There was a horse on a road,
there was the corpse of my father:

was that our love?

Touch these stones,
these shells,

brush the sand from the petals.

Whatever sadness you have
is not our love.

Take the whole orange
and eat it.

*Can there be for lofty natures a purely physical love,
and for sincere natures a love which is purely intellectual?
Can there ever be love without a single kiss,
and a kiss of love without sensual pleasure?
Tell me, what wretched woman has left him with such
impressions of physical love.
Poor angel. They should hang all women who make vile
in men's eyes that which in all creation is most holy
and most worthy of respect, the divine mystery,
the sublimest and most serious act of universal life.
The magnet draws the iron to it....
This is a frightful letter.
It is my ultimatum.*

I said to the man:
there is a black bag,

I am afraid of what you have in it.

I said to the man:
you have a black bag,

I am afraid of what you have in it.

I am finished.
I am made of stone.

You cannot open me up.
Put your knives away in your sack.

I said to the man,
I am finished,
put the stones back
and sew me up.

I said to the baby,
I shall sew you into the sack.

I sewed her up.

Her head broke the stitches.
Her arms and legs broke the stitches.
She ran away.

I said to the man who knocked at the door,
here is a knife.

I said to the angel,
here is a rope.

Cut the baby out,
hang the woman.
I am sick to death
of feeding them.

I said to the angel,
I will feed you.

I said to the man,
I will feed you.

I put the stones in a circle.
I lit the fire.

I stirred the pot of stones
and waited.

If his happiness depends, or is going to depend,
on her,
let him go his way.
If he is to be unhappy, prevent it.
I am ready to sacrifice myself for one I love.

Something is absent.

I check my desk
for books and drawings,

I touch the children's beds
next door;

the closet—my hat, cape, boots,
all are there.

I pick up my walking stick:

the night-table, the music stand,
the piano,

the window, lawn, roadway, stars,

the Mediterranean sea,

the church we did not attend,
the marriage we did not have—

all these are present.

What is it?

I tap my stick.
It becomes a clock.
How long has it been since we met?

I take the horse
and ride to Paris.

I visit all our friends.
There are men, women,
engagements, performances.

There is a boat in a dream.

It travels down a river.
it goes on forever.

What has happened to the Revolution,
to Liberty?

This is not a riddle:

enough blood was spilled
to require an answer.

You must tell me the plain truth.
Don't say a word to the boy [Chopin].
I see only intimate friends, darlings like you,
who have never thought evil of those whom they love.

We shall have comfortable talks
and your depressed spirit will revive in the country air.
If the boy doesn't want to come, leave him alone;

he is afraid of what people might say,
he is afraid of I know not what.

This passion is a country
without any future:

food untasted,
words mistranslated.

The country expands,
acquires new territory:

day-time and night-time
it records a history.

I examine the atlas,
I put a pin on the map

and sent out soldiers.
Some ecstasy,
some tiresome quarrels:

if I knew what to hope for
I should have no more worries,

make jam in the country,
look elsewhere.

In creatures I love
I respect everything I do not understand.
Search in the depths of his soul—
I must know what is going on there.

You know me by heart now.
I send you my warmest regards, dear kind friend.

*I felt I was speaking to my other self,
the best and dearest of the two.*

I come back to the emptiness
inside me,

to the cavity where the baby was,
to the inexhaustible wish to have.

I am extravagant,
yet I live on nothing.

I light one candle.

Now the armies are at the door,

their barges on the river,
their horses covered in blood.

My father died long ago
by a roadside.

I go to the hospital—
the nearby houses are empty—

a soldier offers his pillow.

I touch the bandage,
I help him sit,
I lift his legs up.

He is cold,
his skin prickles.

I lie down with him in my arms.

Tell me what to do,
how to defend him [Chopin].

Chopin's Letters

Love As It Is

I have spoken to the dead.
I have broken my word.
But the dead are all I have.

They ask questions:
where are we?
Are we crossing a bridge?

They are like children.

I look at a tree.
Birds range its branches,
colours slip from lime to silver,

and the dead say, "What is it?"

The bridge moves,
slipping on plates, edging, easing;

the earth turns, and the moon and stars:
they twist free of the hand that spins them.

The dead say, "Are we at rest?"
Yes, and yes.

*I have seen her three more times. It seems
like only a day. She gazed deep into my eyes
while I played...such dark strange eyes she had.
What were they saying? She leaned against the piano
and her eyes seemed to caress mine. I was overcome.
My soul seemed to find its haven in the smile of those
remarkable eyes. I longed for them...my heart
was conquered...I have seen her twice since...
one time alone. She loves me!*

*Aurore! What a charming name! Like the dawn
it banishes darkness.*

July 1838, Paris

Now I will tell you about the voices.
I do not hear them, I speak them.

I speak before I hear.
I do not know what I say, but I am healed
by speaking.

I speak the tongues I reached for.
Through great effort I reached for joy.

Now I do not know what I have,
unless it is praise,
yes, perhaps truly, that is it:

for the exaltation of all gifts,
for the trees especially, and the broad
river of the spirit.

The child looks at the sea and asks if that
is the angel.

It is restless enough.
We look and look at the sea.
We throw stones,
and hold our breath.

I hear the horses shifting their weight
in the field.

I hear the strands of grass rub
the damp earth.

The horses stand as if they belonged,
and could slip across the frost or sun
into forest—

yet they stay.

Their breath is like clouds
of stirring mosquitoes; their heat

flames through the glass.
I put my hand over my eyes and turn back
to my paper.

I write music.

We stand in the field next to the horses.
My joints remember bruises,
the stretch of mounting.

My wrists click as I lift your child.
We stand like drawings.

Palma, 28 December 1838

*or rather Valldemosa, a few miles away; between the cliffs
and the sea a huge deserted Carthusian monastery where
in a cell with doors larger than any carriage-gateway
in Paris you may imagine me with my hair unkempt,
without white gloves and pale as ever. The cell is shaped
like a tall coffin, the enormous vaulting covered with dust,
the window small. In front of the window are orange-trees,
palms, cypresses; opposite the window is my camp-bed under a
Moorish filigree rose-window. Close to the bed is an old
square grubby box which I can scarcely use for writing on,
with a leaden candlestick (a great luxury here) and a little
candle. Bach, my scrawls and someone else's old
papers...silence...you can yell...still silence.*

To Julian Fontana in Paris

I call my mother who made me.
I call my father who made me.
I call the birch trees,
the wind, the snow.
I call the rivers of blood of the moon,
I call the silvery mineral earth,
I call the circle of my childhood,
the horses.

Bind me with their binding.
Bind me with their healing.
Bind me with the circle of love
that is their healing.
I bless the wind for strength.
I bless the snow for music.
I bless the red moon for its dancing movement.
I bless the vegetable earth for its final resting.
I bless the wheel of horses,
I bless the face of a child at a window,
I bless the entry into the circle.

Heal my spirit.

*They tell me that I am better...But I feel that
deep down in myself, something is wrong.
Aurore's eyes are misted: they shine only when
I play, and only then is the world full of
light and beauty...I fear she knows something
about my condition she cruelly keeps from me in
the mistaken belief she is sparing me new pain.*

June 1839

I put my hands in the earth,
I put the earth in my mouth.

I put the sea in my mouth.
I put colour in my mouth.

I light the candle.
A moth swings on the pendulum
of its life.
I trap it and free it.
It comes back.

Knock, knock, goes the wind.
The cypresses scrape the sand.
I read the handwriting:

I run the tap of my blood.

The world is my shadow,
I embrace the light.

Tonight the moon is marvelous.
Never have I seen it like this. But, but!

Please empty my soul of this fear,
please empty my soul of the beating of drums,
please empty my soul of debt,
please empty my soul of disappointment.

Water of the night, the stilling rain,
water of the day, on the tongue,
water of the hour,
water of belief:

I embrace you.

I am living in my cell and sometimes have Arabian dances
and African sunshine. Then there is the Mediterranean. I'm
not sure, but I think I shan't come back before May or even
later. Hand over my letter and the Preludes to Pleyel
yourself.

Write.

To Julian Fontana in Paris
Valldemosa, 22 January 1839

*I feel strange here this year: in the morning I often look
into the room next to mine, but there is no one there...I
keep going into your room and into the one next door where
the Mistress is working—but at this moment I am far away—
as usual in some strange region of space. Of course they are
only those imaginary spaces—but I am not ashamed...I have
written three new Mazurkas....*

*To his family in Warsaw
Nohant, 16-20 July 1845*

My ancestors inhabit my bones.
My bones are like numbers.
My fingers make designs,
I can hear them.

I place my hand on my chest,
I cross the other one over it.
I get no sleep at all.

My heart aches to be opened.
My spirit reaches, and falls back.

Is it tears that I make into music?
You can hear them break, like glass.
I collect them in a vial,
and spill them on paper.

*It is thundery today and rather hot.
The gardener is transplanting flowers.
The giraffe, which I believe Louise and Kalasanty saw, has
died. I wish I never had any sadder news than that to report
to you.*

*I play a little and write a little. Sometimes I am satisfied
with my 'cello sonata, sometimes not. I throw it aside and*

164

*then take it up again. I have three new mazurkas.
When one is doing something it seems all right, otherwise one
would not write anything. It is only later that one reflects
carefully, and either keeps a thing or rejects it.
Time is the best form of censorship and patience the finest
teacher.*

*It is five o'clock and already so dark that I can hardly see.
I must stop now. In a month I shall send more news.*

*To his family in Warsaw
Finished 19th April, 1847*

Dust. Clouds of it that I cough.
A whirlwind, black as a sheath,
a horse snorting foam flecked with blood.

I imagine the sea,
a sweep of meadow decked with bluebells.
You, well, picnicking with children.

They have faces like dishes.
I paint ears on them
and then I listen;

I paint their mouths,
small red bows that open and close,

tongues like smooth ribbon.

I listen: I hear the rattle of teeth,
the intake of breath,

I hear them sobbing as you walk, knee deep
through the grasses, chest deep in the breakers.

I paint it over.
Blue for eyes, this time.

They turn and aim them like bullets,

I paint sunflowers:

they wave at you, swimming.

Parentheses for nostrils,
a handkerchief.

A black cloud swirls in a funnel.
Its cone touches the plate of the earth

and tilts it.

You slip off, in a fall of water
like music.

One need not fully record all that has been said and done. Mme Sand can have nothing but good memories of me in her heart, if she ever looks back on the past...it is a fever for which there is no cure in cases where the imagination is so dominant and the victim is let loose on shifting and uncertain ground. Well, they say "even a cypress-tree may have its caprices."

To his Family in Warsaw
Paris, Christmas 1847

The air moved over her back.
The air that was not air, that was cold,
moved across her shoulder.

She lay sleeping,
golden.

Inside the door,
the door that opened into a cave,

I stood up.
The cold air moved over my arm and shoulder.

I danced to it.
The air swayed away.

Then it fell. The door fell
on my chest, and shut.

If I were made of light, or air,
I would dance,
rise to the rim of the sky,

touch the stars,
fall, all of a piece
on the world.

I would never have left her
for less.

I had thought that a few months spent apart from Chopin would heal the wound, make possible a tranquil friendship, and pour balm on memory. I saw him for a moment in March, 1848. I took his hand. It was as cold as ice, and trembling. I should have liked to talk with him, but he fled. It was my turn to say that he no longer loved me, but I spared him that pain, and left everything in the lap of the gods—and the future. I never saw him again.

George Sand

AUTOBIOGRAPHY

El corriente que nace de esta fuente,
Bien sé que es tan capaz y omnipotente,
Aunque es de noche.
— *St. John of the Cross*

We are the sea's, and as such we are at its beck.
We are the water within the wave and the wave's form.
And little will man—or woman, come to that—
know what he shall dream when drawn by the sea's wrack
*or what he shall hope for once it is clear that he'll never
go back.*
— *P.K. Page*

The Mind's Road to Love

The Mind's Road to Love

1.
In the evening I found you,
a man on a stoop reading

while the life of the forest rose
around him.

In the morning I found you again,
sleeping, while the sun scoured

the hills to brightness,
until at noon I climbed into my spirit.

I saw you through a mirror,
and the mirror was three thousand miles,

and the mirror was a telephone,

but I was blinded by the mirror
and by its shadows,

and I did not see the light of noon
on your face,

I did not find your body in the forest,
or in the sea,

or with my body.

I read all the books,
and I sat on the stoop where I had found you

reading, and I thought of how the books made steps
up a mountain,

and I saw truth in the mirror of words,
and in a face that changed hourly

to a beast, a woman, a man, a child,
to a charitable angel,

to the face of God (He or She) turning away from me.
A ladder fell down from a cloud

as from a spaceship: I began to climb the ladder
rung by rung.

I gave up food and drink,
I took off my wedding ring,

I began to think of the actual
existence of things:

and I saw the species range themselves in order,
with the birds at the top of the ladder,

and at the foot the microbes,
and I saw the human family ascending

and descending as if they were angels,
and the angels were pushed aside,

and I saw that the ladder was a tree in the garden,
and that it required care and feeding and pruning,

and I saw you asleep at the foot of the tree;
and then I saw you speak into the telephone,

and the spaceship descend and the birds feed you.

You looked up. Then the world was made
out of nothing,

but the books described its beauty,
and mathematics measured it,

and with the measuring came power
and lightning, and I flew

to the top of the tree as a bird.
I entered into every species—

human kind ascending and descending,
the great mammals and all the extinct creatures—

the mammoths and the unicorns—
and I made living creatures from stars and stones

and aluminum; I strung telephone wires
and formed networks of fibreoptics,

and lightning made the whole of creation spin,
until it was magnetic,

and the earth attracted the moon and the planets
and I saw the splendor of that whirling,

the turning sea, the spin of blood and fluid
through my body,

the great circle of the trees of the forest,
your arms as they wrapped around me.

But he or she who does not praise is
struck dumb,

so I opened my lips and applied my heart
to my vision of you as it came.

2.
A Reflection on Ecstasy and its Limitation

In the mirror of the actual existence of things
is God,

in so far as He or She has tracked through DNA.
Therefore, in consideration of this, in all creatures

such as you, that enter my mind through my hands and
lips,

through the open nerve ends of the framework of light
in which I walk,

through the electrical nature of the universe,
in you all creatures have entered my heart.

This is the microcosm of which God (He or She) is the
macrocosm,
in which taste is your tongue on mine,

and sight is the cross-hatching of past lives
on the screen of your face,

and sound is the fast falling river that takes the cells
of your skin to my skin,

is the water closing over my head as I open my eyes
beneath you.

This is apparent. Some things are self-generating—
the amoeba and other single-celled creatures—

but others are not.

Even those creatures that engender disease

are beginning lives together,
as is gold, and as is fire,

or the spring bulbs,
as is hydro-electric power.

Ruling over all the elements and creatures are
the animal souls which live through the eyes,

and the librarians' souls which live through
the back of the eyes,

and the souls of the stars and the angels
which are the eyes through which the world

is apprehended and thought.
These move the earth and the planets a little differently

each day: just as my thoughts of you change,
as sometimes they are of God (He or She),

and at others they are like fish slipping

down the melting inside of a frozen waterfall,
as complicated as the process of freezing and unfreezing,

as tricky as looking into your eyes or away from them. These
rulers of which I have spoken

work at their governing.

Then there are the healers. They do not govern,
but stand at the doors of the five senses,

and make apparent the luminous city,
the coloured rainbows, ice, and diamonds

of genuine goodness of the body; they show me the broad
and glorious colours running through you

even as they indicate your magnitude and number. Everything
is moved by something:

I am moved by you.

But I was speaking about the healers
and how they return the sense of delight,

and conjure the scent of roses,

and place bone next to bone,
spleen to spleen—they compare beauties

by reason of proportion so that all is beautiful
when properly placed: I am beautiful

next to you. But theses are only some of the healers.
The others stand at the doors of the senses of

good and evil.

So that I know what is dark and what is light.
I know what is healthful and harmful.

I ask questions about equality:
how we can be the same though we do not change,

how we can pass away into nothing
as if we had walked into the sea,

or set fire to the forest,
or as if we removed ourselves from place and time and motion,

by leaving a restaurant and parting;
or by saying that the eternal light of likeness

and coequal radiance is not God (He or She)
is not even brightness, but is a gold ring

slipped on and off a finger.
But there are laws and certain judgements

just as there is music and steps that mount
from earth to heaven;

and these are the things that I remember,
since they are incontrovertible:

that there are times when you do not love me,
when I am out of step with your reading,

and times when I open the book of the dead and find nothing
but erased pages,

and open the book of the living and see account ledgers with
sums carried forward into forever,

and times when I am poor and in debt and see your shadow your
echo, your picture,

and I place all these things—the shadows and voices
and newspaper photographs—into the fire,

and destroy the world I touch and hear and see,
because I am afraid of being poor and in debt.

Times when I know that this is the end,

and that the angels are not angelic but too much like me, for
every creature has had a photograph taken at some time,

and someone has loved it, criticized it, torn it up.
Even the pictures of love and wisdom, of families.

And there are times when you are unwilling either to be
carried forth from the shadows or to be exorcised, so that

I do not know what to do,

and take the flashlight and shine it on the ashes of the fire,
and piece together the fragments of paper

and make a book of it,
and from the writing of the book I fashion a mirror,

and then a telescope, and I think of everything that exists
in the world and the world beyond

excluding you.

3.
Natural Powers

First we have the water-fall, and then we have the
tides and all the people who have drowned giving off

organic energy,

the ships that slice the waters, the rain as it rises
from the respiring leaves of trees;

then we come naturally to the sun,
and boiling water and the cooking of food,

and the digestive system of the human body,
and we are coming into the inner sanctum

out of which are formed flamenco dancers,
and my friend Mercedes' paintings,

and all the other emblems of power,
Enter then into yourself

and see your mind love itself for its drawings
and typings,

for its choice of shoes with hard heels
for dancing, for the way the eye draws

the body of a loved one, sinuous line by line
all the way to the earth;

and from this be advised that you have natural power.
In the past, perhaps, you have built cabinets,

and cut down the forests that now house you,
and cut down the trees beneath which you read,

and which give you the paper on which you write,
and which make the books that make the steps

to God (He or She): I forgive you all the moments of
inattention. In the present you read and write, and forget

that the muscles of your body were meant for cutting trees in
the morning, and in the afternoon and evening

for holding me—and I forgive you again.

In the future you think of eternal things and of the canopy
of trees that has grown over you,

over the whole vegetable world so that cutting
doesn't come into it, but breathing does,

and rain, and deer stepping through a forest
that turns to minerals in the earth,

and that is mined and placed in nuclear power plants
and is heated and cooled by water;

so that your body is radioactive, and glows and
you become a ladder to the spaceship

and I climb you and we both climb the steps,
affirming or denying as we choose,

recalling that this ladder will take us to God (He or She) or
at least somewhere where we haven't been.

This is the story of my hopes.
As for what I think: I think through the action

of my bones and eyes, that is through the guardians
of all my internal organs

and through the intelligences that stand at the doors
of my senses;

so that I am opening and closing constantly
under their direction,

so that I am constantly choosing and trying to remember
my choices, and trying to discover

where and if and when I said yes to you.
And thus, by so doing, daily,

by making this my prayer, as far as the intellect is
concerned, as far as there is contingent reality

past and present and future,
so far as it is within my natural power

I am with you.

And thus, I am moved,
and I am at least existing,

and I am at least at the time existing with you.
These things follow. This is the truth,

although desire impedes me and my hopes for the future
deceive me: this too is the truth.

So that even when I am running I am existing with you; even
when I am asking

if reaching for happiness is justified,
if human desire, therefore,

seeks nothing but the highest good
or something that leads to it,

or has some resemblance to it...if nothing can be loved
except it is made real

by desire. Because I desire you,
and I desire reality and the image of truth.

In my mind there is intelligence and love,
and these are equals. There is also will,

and there is also the love of God

(He or She) which comes through you: because
you are part of the order of living

and of the spirit of living, and of expression and logic
which are the books (including mathematics) by which

I mount these steps. As if there were a mountain, in truth,
to climb, and not just my separation from you.

It is the vital mystery of ourselves, and our families, the
political structures, and of the illumined birds

that fly up and down the ladders

bringing electronic mail and bread and water
to the human beings who are

thinking of nothing but the blows they have received,
and the animals they have eaten,

and the stars they have numbered like bank accounts:
for they have only their memories

instead of the eyes with which I see you.
And so I bless the irradiated food, the radioactive wastes

of the Arctic seas, because even these illumine
everlasting hills as long as there is you.

4.
Gifts of Grace

It seems amazing that no one else has found you.
Their view is obscured by phantoms, I think,

they have forgotten such sweetness exists;
they do not even have an image of God (He or She),

to help them think about love.
We do not think about love unless we think about truth,

or the tree of life beneath which you read:
we do not think of life after death

unless we think of you or someone like you,
unless there is someone to love forever.

Even when that image is broken,
it is still to be thought of

in its wholeness. Breakage is accidental,
or malicious, it does not matter—

what is broken can be made whole again
if the parts are kept.

The blind are recovering their vision
and the deaf their hearing,

people are looking down from the ladder in fear
and up to the spaceship in wonder:

soon they may turn to you, as if you were God (He or She),
hoping to receive a lesson,

to look upon splendor, to hear, smell, taste and embrace
as they did at first...

but they will not love you as I do.
Because there is dawn and the moon and the sun

like a series of exclamations, because everyone
is different and loves differently,

because the love each has for you
is a descent into the heart through grace,

182

because there are orders of angels
discussing these very matters, coming up with answers,

because we pass through a series of concentric circles,

and touch each other briefly and continue,
because, thanks to God (He or She) I saw you first

and stopped what I was doing.

I was like the law of Nature which purifies an honest life,
and yours was the honest life I discovered.

Now, in these intermediate steps in time, I am proceeding

towards you, creating mirrors for company,
attaching wings for flying, undergoing operations,

if necessary, on my heart, which requires your friendship,
erasing its scars where it lacks feeling,

and reinforcing its steel, so that the things of which I am
ignorant will not break me, so that the spirit

that roots you, that makes me think of God (He or She)
when I think of you, although it judges will not destroy me.

5.
About Your Name

If you wish to think about what is invisible,
you start with a loved one,

with their essence, with the touch of lips
in actuality or in potential: as beginning with

electrons and moving to electricity,
and the hydro electric dams on the rivers,

and the changes of names they undergo
according to politics—that is, you ignore history.

As to the way things are—this is intelligible
only through a vision of you.

Marvellous colours that are invisible except
to the naked eye, unseen by electronic pulses,

or by mirrors, or by angels talking and drawing
each other's pictures,

unseen by all except me, who happened to find you
in the right place and time.

Because when I look at you I seem to see nothing:
I see the sweetness and light that is above

and beyond all mirrors or the hair combing of angels,
or the polishings of motor cars and mountain bicycles:

it is greatest because it is the simplest, and because it is full
like the air, of the intention to touch.

For that which is most actual is you when I see you
and when I am with you.

You ask how this came about:
it is a question of grace, not practice,

a step in the right direction by chance,
a desire, not thought.

And I meditated on the mind's ascent to love
the whole world before me, and all the roads,

and I waited for you.

Nature's Children

...should you, that have the governance
Of Nature's children, heaven and earth throughout,
Prescribe them rules, and live yourselves without?

— Sir John Davies

*Que bien sé yo la fonte que mana y corre,
Aunque es de noche.*

— St. John of the Cross

Nature's Children
   for Patrick Lane

We left the house in the dark.
No one saw us go. We held hands,

for fear of being lost. There was no moon,
no light with us but the night itself:

we followed it
from the narrow roadway that led to the city,

into the blackness of the fields

where the animals moved silently,
their feet muffled in earth,

their horns tangled in dead stars,
their fur brushed dull with the ashes of the dead.

Withheld breath, the astonished silence
of stifled hearts, gave direction;

and still we followed what we saw,
the darkness rising.

I could see your face for the first time,
its look of age, the tired eyes,

the sadness of eternity,
its knowledge of love.

I could hear the passage of night,
of lost animals, of falling trees.

I could smell blood,
and it was also the sweet salt of the sea.

You lay face down on the earth.
I could see your skull as it would be in a century,

the shape of a man remaining for study,
the penis and testicles like plants;

the lungs were fungi, the organs like separate
jewels, the impression of a skeleton

no more than a leaf-print.

I saw that you were a shadow,
and the body in which I had believed,

and the pain that had given it shape,
disappeared into the warp of eternity.

I wanted the suffering
that had given me your body,

I wanted the journey, the stones,
the appalling cries of the desperate.

I wanted nothing else
except death to unmake me,

and restore us—

as you stepped to the entrance of a sea cave,
as you saw me deep in my listening,

and decided
not to be

alone.

Autobiography

Autobiography

1.

i. I was born
in a caul.

I was proof
against drowning.

Green marble and a gold locket
were placed with the caul in my basket:

flecks of white foam in the green,
a gold penis, a gold sun on a chain;

the skin was the stretched white
of an egg.

They put my head in a bucket of water.
The villagers watched. I breathed water like sunlight,
the light I was born with. Gold.

I had a red thread around my waist.
The caul was folded, dried like snake-skin,

tied with the thread.

ii. I was found
in the cork tree at the bridge.

A man drove his truck over the bridge and parked it next
to the river. His tire tracks

made the long thin cries of a wounded animal
in the red earth. He took his wide

knife and began to cut the bark.
He finished cutting

and stuck the knife in the body of the tree. (He tells me
this as he stares in a scrap of mirror,

picking his teeth. He touches the blood on his gums
with his finger.)

I was high in the branches
with my empty infant face.

There was milk on my shift,
a wrap of dirty cloth between my legs.

(He says he saw, for an instant, the face of an angel.)
The sun drew the shape of a small gold figure.

I can remember,
deep in my blackness,

a rainbow as it danced into my eyes. My pupils swallowed
her. She remained, a mannequin, in my brain.

(I wear a white cloth over my eyes.
My eyes are colourless film.)

The man wept at the sight of the angel.
He had discovered his sins. They were in his hands,

his mouth, his feet, the gold penis that dangled
between his legs. They were

in water, the thread of blood he drew
on my skin with a knife.

They were like brilliantly coloured beads,
fragile, made of glass.

He placed them, loose, in his pocket.
I stirred in my basket.

I could smell the pines
and the rust of the cut cork trees.

The tree trembled.
The man saw light and shadow.

iii. When I was three years old
the man showed me the coloured glass beads.

I played with them while he slept.
I made circles,

bodies of men and women, a head with all-seeing
eyes.

I felt his sins.
I held them to my eyes, but saw nothing.

I put them in my mouth and breathed in colours and sunlight.
I breathed, with his breathing, the silent light,

the scaly lids of his eyes. I breathed amber
and smoke, the strangled cries of afternoon bells,

the goat limping down the path.
I put the glass beads back.

In church, on Sundays, I sat in the pew with the villagers
and felt shadows climb the thin walls of my legs.

I could hear the shores of the cork grove by the river,
the fall of bark, its blood soaking into the ground.

I bit my thumb. I put the green marble in my mouth.

I felt the flecks of milk,
I touched the wrapped caul,

the red thread,
the gold locket.

iv. When I was twelve
I was baptised.

I walked to the river behind the minister.
I wore a white slip.

There was no one with us. But when we came to the riverbank,
the cork-cutter waited beside his truck. The minister's wife

was at home, sick, lying back in her bed, her dress drawn
above her knees.

I had heard her thighs, like two animals,
hungry pieces of flesh;

I had heard the minister's words to God
fall like bright coins into empty pockets.

He stood still with his hand on my back.
We had entered the river. The flat of his hand

was a stone. I sank to the bottom. My hair followed
the current. My hair was a still brown fish. The minister

caught it and lifted me up. The cork-cutter stayed where he
was; I could feel his sharpness.

A woman came across the bridge.
Soon I walked beside her in the dust.

- I carried skins of water.
At night she let me warm myself at the fire.

High in the rose-coloured mountains
where the houses sat like white teeth,

she picked some herbs.
I drank the tea she made from them,

and I could see.

2.

I know that by these few [remarks], I am providing not only starting points but conclusive proofs to those in whom inwardly there blazes fiery strength and a heavenly origin, so that they may indeed readily lend their ear to the great Democritus, announcing to those who wish to effect a healing of the soul and a deliverance from all distress that this doctrine is not mythical, but mystical and arcane; as also [they may listen] to that [author] who has asserted that the logos of the creative universe works by rules so that man, godly-minded and born of God, may learn by straight-forward work and by theological and mystical language.
— John Dee

3.

i. The appearances began soon after her death in 1962. They occurred firstly in the street near her home. Two women

saw her come to the window and knock to be let in.
We are driving down an endless road into the desert. It is

nighttime, but I can feel the heat frozen in the chevy frame.
I have my feet on the hump in the back seat. My friend, Dan,

taps his fingers on the steering wheel.
He is listening to music.

Beside him the medium is quiet. The bulk of her teased hair
rises above the headrest. We carry food, water, blankets,

candles, rice and salt for the ritual. I have a green stone
in my pocket. Suddenly, the car swerves and we slide across
the road.

The stars, bright as cat's eyes, ride the arc above the
flatness. Jesus! Dan gets out of the car.

He walks to the front and kicks the tire. I open the door.
The air is cool. "Someone will be along to get us," I say,

looking down the empty road. There is no one. He sticks
his hands in his pockets. He is a long lean man with
straight

grey-black hair—an airline mechanic. He is due back at
work tomorrow. "We're on the right road," he says. I look
down the road.

I can feel the strain of watching nothing. "Should we do
something?" I ask the medium. She shrugs and tucks herself

into the blanket. I fall asleep and when I awaken I feel
something cold in my chest. I try to move,

but I can't.

ii. We run out of water and drink from the radiator. There
is so little. I don't mind, but I wanted to see her. She

sits in my mind like a foreign country.
She would cure me if I could touch her.

Sweetheart.

iii. I go to the King
show him the caul,

the red thread,
the locket of gold.

I tell him about the cork tree,
the wind stirring rainbows.

He touches me all over.

We go to the church and do penance.
For seven years I live in the desert without him.

My hair grows long. I am brown as earth.
I try to drown myself in a well, but the water won't take me.

I belong to the earth.
I return to the King.

4.

I would have wept if weeping
netted continents in heart's safekeeping:
what do you want, why call or write
to me? My heart's closed, it's night,
my hand will never trace your cheek in sleeping.

As dawn began its walk, its sweep
of all good sense, you took my hand: fleeting
touch that left its mark—I feel it yet—why should I fight
to lie to you? I would have wept.

There are no words for this regret, a leaking
hard, dry as drought, unstaunched by all these months: needing
you is all it is, a wound against myself, slight
as a sting of frost or second-sight—
I have no heart for change, no grieving (understand?)—
But, oh, I could have wept.

5.

I remember, first, the surgeons, dressed in green
hospital gowns, masked, wheeling intravenous carts through
the street. There were a dozen or so of them moving across
the square. Next, half a dozen 'traffic-lights', their heads
encased in cardboard boxes of flashing lights; a woman
dressed as a shower, her flesh-coloured body-stocking showing
through a transparent plastic curtain, and the chrome shower-
head pointing down at her from above. I remember carrying my
daughter because she was afraid of the noise and people, and
a period where I could no longer carry her and Kevin held both
children on his shoulders, biceps straining the sleeves of
his shirt, the tendons in his neck as thick as the spines of
books. He and Angelica—thin, quick, pretty with her long
dark hair—seemed like dream figures, companions to whom I
was attached—I had forgotten why—until the sun rose or I
died. Both seemed equal possibilities, because of the fever
I didn't know I had.

    In the café on the square, to which we returned for
the second time to buy juice for the children, my daughter
and I waited to use the bathroom. After fifteen minutes in
line we went in. The bowl was smeared with shit. There was
shit and water on the floor. She looked at me, "Mummy, what
will I do?"

    "I'll hold you, honey." There was a noise in my ears
like the sea. Planes passing overhead from the base at
Rota.

The five of us in one room, in Cadiz.

6.

Awakening in time

to see the rooms bright with moonlight
spread in sheets, folded in corners.

Awakening, fingers wet, wet mouth,
sweat painted like gold

on flesh,

to hear silence
anonymous as the weather,

and understand
it's not enough

to ask for more
time in the hourglass:

like Dante's continents, we are hell
and heaven in the same body,

the fingers and the mouth,
the sleepy puckered flesh, the mind

on its long stroll;

the moonlight as it was when you awoke
on the dark side of the world, spinning

towards sunrise.

How Were The People Made?

On the Making of People

after "How Were the Glass Flowers Made?", a letter by Mary Lee Ware, Botanical Museum Leaflets, Harvard University Vol. 19, No. 6

I have been out to Woodside, forty minutes by car,
alone, four times and have passed whole afternoons,

long ones, looking at the tiny people ready for shipment
or placement.

I inspected the work room in the house,

viewed the billiard room and the pool

and all the other improvements made by the Cooks
since their marriage, and finally accepted their hospitality

of tea and afternoon biscuits. A far better arrangement than
spending a whole day and taking two solid meals

(you know what they are like)
as before.

Both Mr. and Mrs. Cook greeted me at the gate,
and we looked at each other to see what time had

accomplished.

He must have dropped nearly a foot in height,
and his hands were trembling so that I wondered if the work

had become too much.

However I decided that this was due to anxiety
as to what I should say about the prototypes.

He has been working evenings, sometimes by starlight.
I remonstrated vigorously and told him he must not do so:

you cannot always be sure of the result when he's tired. But
he only said that you wanted the models at once,

that it was impossible to work any faster,
that nobody could.

He regrets that all the groups of heads
are not complete: but he has had to do them as he could,

and when he could get the specimens.

However, teeth, eyes, thighs, rib-cages, hearts and livers
are for the most part finished, ready for the varnish, with
the colours

set to paint, and the exquisite breasts ready for the chests.
The feet are not so beautiful to look at,

but they are marvelous, and how one man can sit, hour after
hour, putting in the gossamer veinlets,

or all the myriad little dots of the pores, irregular brown
patches, spots and sores, passes my understanding.

If he hurried
or worked quickly, he would be insane.

The workroom table is covered not only with saws, scalpels,
scoops, glues and so on, but with trays of fingers,

sculpted but not painted, bottles in which he can stand
the stems of eyelashes while drying or cooling,

specimens of all kinds to be used as guides,
bottles with voices of all timbres as required,

saucers for the flush of emotion (quickly spoiled).
In spite of the slightly unsteady hand,

his movements are deft, soft in laying down cells, or taking
up hairs: the umbilici are

a performance in themselves—speed or a miscalculated
movement might ruin the work of hours: each wrinkle

each knot and tie are a miracle.
The genitalia also are good, the pudendum like

peaches; the phalli seemed to me less so, but
the final varnish was not on, and they all looked

rather glassy. It leaves you breathless
that anyone can and will do such work.

And now a word about his methods.

Each square of skin is formed of clear plastic,
pulled and stretched by simple instruments over

a burner. Then he pricks it all with sand-paper
to give the right texture. The skin remains

attached to a frame of glass until the colouring
is finished. Then it is separated and is ready

to be attached to the skeletal frame already constructed.
You will appreciate that these are tiny creatures:

one completed could stand in the palm of your hand,
yet they are animate: you should hear them weep

when I leave: several have fallen in love with me,
which makes staying over night in the house, or solitary walks,

next to impossible. There have been incidents,
but I have brushed these aside in the general interest.

It took from about three till half past five to colour
just three patches of skin and put them over a section of

muscle and vein, and then attach the nerves so that
they responded.

The colours are made of pigments taken from stone:
he grinds them himself, even (if his wife is to be

believed)
quarries the rock by hand.

Add a few drops of fluid, carefully milked, and stirred into
the powder in china saucers, and there you are.

A strip of pointed whale bone marks the main veins,
the pointed quill of one of the brushes stresses the ribs

with fractures. Healthy parts are rose-tipped, less healthy
yellow and black and so on.

Then, with the most delicate touch, cob-web lines are drawn
on at the eyes, almost more

delicate then the membranous egg sacs in the females,
and absolutely exhausting to the nerves and patience.

He took a glass stem in his left hand and inserted it beneath
the heart: you could hear the organ gasp,

it was then I began to believe it would work.
I saw one creature stir and sit (Cook keeps his right hand out

to manipulate and guide): it turned and twisted to get free,
but he held it firm. Sometimes they break,

so a great many parts are necessary to complete even one.

Most of the people are finished and quantities of spare
limbs, eyes, internal organs (complete to ovaries and testes)

lie waiting for painting in drawers. They are like
eggshells: too perishable for transport. But he is

confidant that the completed models will survive if they are
shipped by pinning the necks onto cardboard,

and he has ordered a very heavy weight for the boxes.
This has been a long letter and I shall be very eager

to know if you receive it safely. I am going to rest now
before lunch.

Please send someone else in my place
if I don't come back,

and have the Cooks punished.

How Were the People Made?

*:in which the author replies to the Bible, Darwin and Mr. Emery,
her grade six school teacher.*

i. *they were made with sticks*

They were made with sticks,
they were made with mud.

They were made with brooms in their hands,
with carpenters' aprons,

they were made with nails in their pockets,
with bread dough rising under their armpits,

they were given cherries for breasts,
rolled leaves for scrotums,

crows to shadow them,
shadow shadow

crows to remind them.

They were made with leaves,
with a spiral of smoke from

a cigarette; they were made with
springs from old beds,

they were made with rats to run
over them, with tea leaves,

eleven times strained; they were made
with a cough, an ache in bones,

with a cry captured in the palm
of their hands. They were made

huddled together, they were made lonely
at night when the stars

sang. And sang numbers, scales
of geometry, progressions of positives,

precipitation of crystals, the diamond
tuning fork of the mind.

Intellect. Intellect.

ii. they were scraped together from shavings

They were scraped together from shavings,
scraps of sand and mouse dung,

they were swept up, piled, until heat
set them ablaze, until they were ash

and clay, until they fell into good hands,
were useful, paid their way

as cups, water jugs, plates, vases,
chess pieces, pregnant goddesses,

until they were shattered, buried
geological eons below the sprung couches,

the cardboard boxes in which infants
play and are buried;

below discarded cheeseburgers and sprite
lids,

below disposable needles and diapers,
below stars cut from tin,

flowers twisted from charred ends
of dresses, women's dreams, their colours,

distance travelled by men, moving their
families, looking for work...

falling slowly inward toward the earth's
iron core

until my spoon struck gold and scooped them out.

iii. they were made with ships to sail

They were made with ships to sail,
rope to burn their hands,

scars to inflict on knees
and cheekbones,

they were made old with poor food,
well with cod liver oil,

they were made with land,
forest paths,

stockades and forts,
they were made with chance encounters,

a whistle to call companions,
time on their hands,

they were made to wait
for a farmer to forget the barn door,

for a horse to pull its tether,
for a wind that cried, you!, pointing

at them, for a girl and a boy to get away,
evade capture, gather sweet

grasses, tend each other.

iv. they were made with a blanket of stars

They were made with a blanket of stars,
they were drawn across the universe

until they were in shreds.
They were made to open their eyes

in moonlight, they were forced to watch
starshells and artillery bursts,

they were ordered to re-define light.
They were wired up to EEGs,

they were cross-referenced with earthquakes,
they were put to sleep with pills,

they were cornered in garages, they closed
the doors, turned on the engine,

they were found, just in time,
they were fed liquids, they were taught

two syllables, *yes*, and *but*,
they were given flesh in which to carve,

initials, they ate meat until they felt
pain,

they were strapped in electric chairs,
they signed confessions,

they lit candles, they organized choirs
of dissenters, they returned the dead

to the underworld, they opened the tombs,
they unburied the children,

they glued together bones,
they constructed brains of crepe paper,

they made repairs to lakes and mountains,
they closed bomb shelters and opened

shelters for women, they found a single cell
of gold, a scraping from an angel's fingernail,

they knew what it was, but could not remember,
they heard a heart, somewhere, they knew what it was

but could not remember,
they smelled cold air, snow,

they smelled birth, they could not remember
much except for a paw print,

something passing by them, passed by.
gone.

v. they were made with fire

They were made with fire.

vi. they were made with a series of doors

They were made with a series of doors:
yellow, blue, green and red.

They were made with entrances.
They were made with hands to turn handles,

feet to step over sills,
eyes to be astonished,

mouths to praise.
They were made with earth, water, light and time.

They were made with a meeting,
a second third and fourth chance;

they were made with grievous partings,
tears for writing, stone to etch on,

they were made with reunions,
with the memories of past lives,

with answers;
they were made with pain

and the ability to bear it;
they were made with love—

they could give it up, anytime,
They were made to take chances,

they were made to ride unicorns, eagles,
baba-yaga's chicken house,

they were made to touch the thin glass
of existence, and not break it.

They were made to solve problems,
they were made to listen.

vii. they were made like someone

They were made like someone
who hears a name.

viii. they were made from a schoolroom

They were made from a schoolroom.
They were made from flashcards

and enough correct answers.
They were made from spelling bees,

a few unexplained absences at recess
and lunchtime,

in the woods where the horses were tethered.
They were made from doctors and nurses,

from a list of food rules,
from a book that said never to touch the genitals.

They were saved by out-door cookouts,
and singalongs, they were saved by secret

car rides round the lake, at night,
they were saved by laughter,

they were saved by the right person at the right time
in a Madrid taxi,

they were saved by the touch of a hand
that reminded them

whose body it was, whose desire,
whose need to put the separated heart

together. They were made from bivalves.
They were made from an indivisible whole.

They were made from pictures that were altered,
and altered again.

They were made from paintings
by a child with an imaginary friend.

They were made from a single shoe in the middle of the road.
They were made from expectations.

ix. they were made between two riders

They were made between two riders.
They were made in the moving space

between eight hoofbeats.
They were made in the distance between

two sets of invincible armour.
They were made at the point of two lances,

the conjunction of rays on the retina,
twice.

They were lifted, they ran faster than they'd
deemed possible:

they could keep up, they felt the web of light
and dark support them,

they didn't mistake them for wings;
they smelled the sea as they tracked its edges,

they didn't mistake it for life;
they saw the sun set, the moon rise,

they made no mistakes, they shot no predators,
they harmed no strangers,

abandoned no babies,
memorized no Dante;

they moved along the earth, through the sky.
Amen. Amen.

x. how were the people made?

they were made with sticks
they were scraped together from shavings

they were made with ships to sail
they were made with a blanket of stars

they were made with fire
they were made with a series of doors

they were made like someone
they were made from a schoolroom

they were made between two riders

Mirror Gazing

"...their thoughts trembled
between moments of estrangement and ecstatic moments

of reconciliations, and their desire
crucified itself against the unutterable

shadow of silence."

— Hamish Henderson, 'Third Elegy'

You have your cup of coffee
at a white table in the kitchen,

the blank screen of the sky,
the white screen of the sun is behind you.

You have the whole pale morning.
The story you have yet to write

is of a boy walking in sand.
He stumbles, not on the body of his dead sister,

but on a fossil—a sea creature feeding on an eternity
of sea dried-to-stone.

He finds the stone that is the missing history of the earth
as you drink your cup of coffee,

and your body finds its outline
against the screen of sky,

a meeting of forest and desert,
the flesh of a girl in sand.

The wind lifts strands of her hair.

"The nervous fingers of the searchlights
are nearly meeting and time is flickering."

(Hamish Henderson, 'Opening of an Offensive')

*There, it is cooler still. White-walled tires,
the deep pitted black of the chasis,*

*a green lawn-mower next to the garage wall,
the rake, my father's red tool chest,*

*my mother's emerald ring, caught in a clump of garden earth:
I hear field mice,*

*the sugary creep of ants,
the car engine,*

*the door slam, feel the wheels as they roll,
my body like sponge.*

First, before taking another step,
I must find you, my dream children.

You were taken from me by a bandit.
He hides in the darkness.

I am not counting the bones he has placed
in the walls,

nor examining their patterns,
the skulls, like crotchet hooks,

I am not cataloguing

a circle of suns and moons,
tables where grace is said—

I find you, children,
as you roll down a green hill

like coloured glass bulbs
in scales of unbreakable laughter.

You cry out, Mother—watch us!

The red eyes of a rat swallow you,
the bandit makes you dance in his stomach—

but the green hill exists, that is all that counts.

I have a moment to love you,

as the rat gnaws the gold posts of the world
to four small red bracelets.

There is a small girl dressed in red,
red socks and shoes, a red dress,

red underpants.

She turns her head like a cat.
She opens her mouth.

Inside it is a cave, a story of angels,
inside is a map.

She is at the gate where she must go.
Are you lost?

She looks round. No, I am not dead, she says.
There are hundreds of dead children on my planet,

and they all wear red.

Children in trance,
their blue and white nightgowns

billowing in drafts of heated air,
hands outstretched

as they walk the hot coals of the fire in the cauldron.
This came to me in a dream, and through the eye

of a red stone.

I thought of Ceridwen's cauldron,
but mine was forged from copper, and it burned.

If I awaken them, they may feel pain.
But the green stone shows

they walk on water,
float over mountains.

Speak to them in their language
and they cry, We are sailing home!

Dark clouds gather
a spiral of wind.

Can you hear me?
I can hear and touch you.

Your sleeping-walking hands.

✧

*Time is a red stone.
I listen to its track*

*along my father's bare arms,
the red sleeve line,*

*a chewed match-stick between his lips,
yellow pencil behind his ear,*

*sweat stains of his hat-band,
a carpenter's apron with seven pockets,*

four types of nails, a plumb-bob, tape, nail punch.

*I see the light angel and the dark.
Which, which?*

✧

When I speak to you
about the red room

and the woman striking her fists on its walls,
I want you to remember

a child shut in the closet.
I want you to hear her conversation,

watch her walk through the snow
of her heart,

record her farewell to all she has known and loved.

We have waited
for her footsteps to creak

along the crystalline path,
to sound through emptiness.

I want you to hear her as she
turns to watch the woman

hitting the blank red walls of herself.

I want you to say to them both,
Look, there is a door, open it.

Cold air blows over the threshold.
It doesn't matter, nothing matters. *Open it!*

The child steps forward, turns the handle,
and the two, like some image

from Bedlam—pale, gaunt, deranged—
emerge to

a snowstorm of music.
They listen through chattering teeth and lips,

they drink it like soup.

I wait for you every day.
Every day I say your name.

At 2:00 you come,

I go down the steps
to the lawn.

You pick dandelions,
search in the grass,

find a buttercup.

You love butter, you say. I just knew.
My hand shakes as I pick a flower.

You too.
You stand, brush off the grass, vanish.

If I could see the yellow light
like a cup of spring water, like a new brain,

find the light in my bones, the new water,
the cup to hand over, full to the brim,

say, Take it. Don't wait. Do it now.

✧

You were my first, imaginary, lover.
Do you remember the slipcover of dark,

the square of window in my room,
the creak of the oak tree beyond?

An owl waited for the first mouse
as I said your name.

I can see the thin cord from the lamp,
my sandals in the closet,

the easel beside the bed,
the book of poems.

You said, wait. And got up,
creaked open the door to the kitchen,

where my parents sat at a table, talking,
holding hands, crying.

We lay in the quiet,
while I travelled the whole long road

of my life.

Now I can feel you gather the violets,
roses, daffodils, the green branches of thyme—

our private language of hope.
You are here in each cell of darkness.

I can see the small boat waiting,
feel it tremble as we both

step in, set out.

My brother lies in his bed,
the corners of the room, like the outer stars,

send unreadable dim messages.

Milky light pooled on the floor,
the long stripe of wall,

two cars an hour, at most, pass by.
Fruitbowl lamp, string-tied pyjamas,

teeth like rows of fisheyes tied to spoons,
he casts and reels in silence.

✧

You paint the dark walls of your room white,
then you crayon on colour—

a tree, a house, mountains,
the far away Pacific.

You draw until the woods disappear,
the dead animals, the birds' feathers,

cat entrails, the opaque eye of a squirrel.

You draw families of mother, father, sister,

brother, with pets.
Mothers in aprons, fathers in hats,

brothers holding your hand. You draw
until the snowy sky clears, the silver clouds

unleaden, the child tied to the tree
is released. You draw over the boys with the pellet

gun, over what you saw when you followed them,
over what you did not do, how you did not help.

You colour in rainbows across the distance you've dropped.
You draw and draw

until one day you start again to paint the woods,
the three boys with the gun, blood on the crows,

the cat's slit stomach.
You paint snow falling on the child tied

to the tree, paint his screams
as they shoot him, paint it all, hide nothing.

Paint back the cruelty until you see
it is true, there was nothing you could do

but let the feathers and bones
fly free, bless them, bury them,

mark them in memory.

A tub of light below the streetlamp,
Uncle Jim's bicycle rotates

out of seaside fog. dark spokes,
balloon tires, half way in and out.

*Katy's bosoms are silver and gold
in the open shelf of her raincoat.*

*He stops, removes the cap that tops
the metal plate in his skull,*

*opens his pension book. He is late home
to his sister three straight nights,*

*then he's wed.
Kent, that's where he went, for brides,*

*there were none in Canada half as convenient,
as Elsie, Katy, or the last wife whom no one liked.*

I remember how

*long we had to wait, my mother and I, before she
opened the door to our knock,*

*took my mother aside
to ask about Jim, where he spent his time,*

*his bank accounts. She had bad teeth
a nice smile between her bow and arrow lips.*

She gave me sweets, there was a smell of sex

*and drink in each. There was none
of that at home, nylon brush sofa, green arborite,*

*an extra leaf in the kitchen table on Saturday night.
We tipped our chairs back on two legs*

for excitement.

Katy, Katy, Jim sang Beautiful Katy *for you, the second wife,
in the grim brown apartment. You had cleaned the fridge,*

made tea and shortbread biscuits, I ate two
and watched your eyes, like batteries

flashing lights, you liked it here, liked Jim;
he never told us how or when you died.

Mirror Gazing
for Pepe

I did not ask the dead to come,
they came anyway,

the uncles, fat as sea-lions,
the aunts, patting waved hair.

Shadows of dust, their hands neatly stowed
in pockets,

they made a garden of themselves
beyond the black gate,

gathered like fallen leaves, stiff dry branches,
a forest floor of twigs and nettles,

skins a net for spores,
eyes a map of webs.

How they passed through,
brushed their way down damp earthings,

stumbled from tunnels, slipped the lock.
I did not ask.

They were a mist of unburnished thought,
smudged with static,

knew nothing but dust,
were voiceless,

half-erased.

Yet I knew the place they meant—beyond the wood

where in the dark

we pass along the shore, arms red
in torchlight, the splintered steps of

adults, stopped, the children quiet as grass, tongues cut
loose from chains, and shiver in the wind,

mute with chill, tap a lover's wrist three times for luck,
to start again.

Interior Castle

Interior Castle

*"Ancient shipwrecked cities
tell us of the omnipotence of Silence,
of her sudden overwhelming floods within their walls;
the snows of time are heaped on her breast;
in a slow movement voyaging,
the icebergs of millenniums proceed..."*
        — Melissánthi, from "Ancient Shipwrecked Cities"

Let us imagine the heart as a castle,
and the world as a castle

with many mansions.
You must think of this each day,

in your heart, in silence. You must recall
differences: how a door opens and closes,

and no one slips through; how a door shuts
on the imploring hand reaching through it,

and you feel no pain,

how a door slams in the wind *north east south west*
how every direction is against you

as you move from room to room, mansion to mansion,
world to world;

how the wind that blows death into your mouth,

that makes you push your fists into your eyes
like a child and gasp at pain, light and food,

gasp at love, each time it is offered and withheld,

how that wind is a man or woman you love,
who is taken from you at the beginning of time

as you lie in the sand with a thousand
anonymous creatures waiting for thought,

for the wind to drive the sea into its canyon,
for cells to join and die in their millions,

and ponds to engender egg, larvae, a deep
layer of striding insects,

for a phone to ring,
a man to get in his car,

an airplane to imprint its cross
on the blank film of the sea-bed,

burst open,
seed,

to lie in emptiness thousands of miles away
listening to the guttering of breath,

the slow undertow of souls,
the silence of the closed-off rooms of your heart:

so that underneath the brilliance of
stars among the waves of darkness,

the earth among the waves, crumbled and raised, ascended, and descended,

one more door would open and close
to bring you in from the waves.

We might say that union is as if the ends of two wax candles were joined so that the light they give is one: the wicks and the wax and the light are all one; yet afterwards the one candle can be perfectly well separated from the other and the candles become two again, or the wick may be withdrawn from the wax...."
— St. Teresa of Avila

Let us imagine the heart as a castle.
Let us imagine its rooms:

and the poor active souls—good neighbours,
miracle workers, reader of good books, good people

who come through sickness and trials;
sisters, those who owe favours and repay them,

who respond immediately to your telephone calls,
those who wait for days

for you to answer, who persevere,
who have good desires—

who ask entry.

In this entrance room of the heart
you never leave me.

Then there is the room where I lose my life.

Then there is work and perfect practice.

There are the hidden things,

dark roads and whirlwinds, the locked
organs of the body and the keys of it scattered

mindlessly, wastefully;

the room where an infant scrawls on a blackboard,
the room where teachers decipher God,

the room where a janitor drinks whiskey,
and places his calendar so the children can see

the upside down head with the hair
falling across the proscenium of

the pelvic arch, the impossible desire to *look*
and *see*,

the room where I said this is forever,
felt the tides

as you left, drawn away, by the deepest of
your desertions, your death.

"But here it is like rain falling from the heavens into a river or a spring; there is nothing but water there and it is impossible to divide or separate the water belonging to the river from that which fell from the heavens. Or it is as if a tiny streamlet enters the sea, from which it will find no way of separating itself...."
—St. Teresa of Avila

Before earth and water find their nests,
before the city is built

and sails forth;
before earthquakes, and killed meat,

the stripping of minerals; and tempered glass
towers that mirror firstly sky,

then the deep chasms drawn through the brain
by the half-light of an architect's pencil,

and ancient ley lines, paved; before the migration
of caribou fenced, re-directed, then eliminated,

and landscapes that heave with underground silos,
and engineered food,

with exhausted souls
and their plunder,

I am grieving for you,
anchored in eternity

(before the shipwreck, the plane crash,
the event),

grieving because I remember,
and can't forget.

She Goes Away
for P.K. Page, and in memory of Sarain Stump

She sets a stone against the door.
She goes away,
"spreading out her arms as birds do their wings."

She goes away to the land of the dead.
Blue lips touch her ankle. Her pulse is a stone
falling into the mouth of a human face.

For Death there is no remedy,
for Life, much to do.
Put on your clothes, let's go to your father.
He hasn't yet lit the candles.

It is dark at the entrance,
there are shadows at the back door.
In the middle of the night someone will ask,
Who is there to love me?

⟡

In the dark mountains,
where no rooster crows,
only the ghosts sing, three hours before daylight.

One song for the morning, another for mid-day,
another for the night beyond the earth,
below sunlight.

⟡

Come to me,
on a dark night,
leave the window open.

No dog will hear us,
no rooster will crow.
My name is in the dark night.

Let us go to the sea,
and leave nothing behind,
not even a footprint to lead to the waves.

⟡

What will they hear
when they bathe with the horses, put their ears in the sea,
shake them?—

The children in the sand,
and sailors, far away,
opening closed doors.

Better to have died
without pain,
apparently only asleep,
at the door, ready to leave,

before the messenger came

Sisters,

I will make you
a thin waist,
skin,
a skin like rose petals,
eyes,
eyes that could break glass....

Nothing more. I won't keep you

WHEN I AM DEAD AND MY HEART IS WEIGHED

Emblems

Dog

When I am dead,
someone will weigh my heart.
It will be Anubis,

or, with luck, my old dog, Grainne,
who will gaze at the golden scale,
add a feather so they'll let me in....

Grainne licked the salt from my legs
as I sat at the kitchen counter
and paid bills, or wrote poems:

the trees shone with rain, my friends slept off drink
in those times, when my heart was done up tight,
like a piece of store meat,

so that I would not feel
the slow leak.
Yet...

sometimes I danced,
held the dog's paws to my chest, for pure joy.

If I am lucky, when I am dead and my heart is weighed,
Grainne will be there,
to say that I danced with her.

and that she lay at the bedroom door
while I crept in secretly
to touch the hand,
the soles of the feet,

and lay my cheek to my mother-in-law's cheek.
How beautiful she was—how thirsty for life
when she died.

I did not say goodbye
until that night, someone knocked on the walls,
furniture fell, a voice cried out

to the stars, straight up, above the bed.

I dropped like a stone into after years
as the spirit of la belle mère fled.

I could not bear to be alone, in those times.

And now, I am alive, and dream of a house
with open windows,
and footprints on the sills,

and the coming in,
and the going out.

Apple

i.
I open the door to the bedroom.
I can smell your sweater, the warm leather of your shoes,
the heat of your ironed shirt at the moment
you undress and come to bed.

A single hair whitens the pillow, and I wonder where
you have gone.
There is nothing to touch, but a child cries,
and an old man is angry at whoever I have become.

Hold your breath, it will soon be over:
you will be as you were before, breathing
at the door of the room of someone you love.

ii.
I open the door to the bedroom.
The covers are thrown back, the sheets clean.

I sit carefully on the edge. You reach for me,
your skin a soft beige glove, wrinkled from handling.

There is sky and the textile earth outside,
and down the hall, a torn shower curtain.

If I hold my breath it will be as it once was,
when I placed my mouth—just so—to taste
a boy I loved;

and he took an apple
split it with his thumbs,
and let me lick them.

Father

You rise, ghostly father,
like a tenant in the basement, who comes
from below, his beer bottle half full,

his mind jammed with scores—
he has forgotten of what—
forgotten what he had to say, and was urgent,

stands grinning, fly undone,
rent unpaid, in a suit from the Sally Ann—
its soup stains and semen, broken glass in the pocket—

the back door left open to the winter wind,
sleet blowing under the door,

his eyebrows white, stiff with surprise, at these
        broken   bylaws

(a lawnmower blade turning, slowly, over the earth
through thick, wet grass.)

Mercury

A knot, clear silver, where a louse sits
    pooling mercury near the skull.

These poor constellations...
    sprinkled like teaspoons of sugar
    in a net!

My child's starry scalp is oceanic,
makes deep work for fingers finding light.

No better way but to
    lose myself
in busy work.

The philosophers egg (maybe)
by hand.

Self

Sometimes I forget all about myself. The world
is suddenly far away, no longer inside me.
That I am alive, has surprised me.
How many birds have sat in this orange tree?
How many children have stolen the fruit?
When I was a bird myself I could have told you.
My hands have spread the stars across the heavens. Yes,
since you ask, I am close to God.

A young man calls to his wife while their unborn child
listens: "Today I will be in the garden, come and find me.
You will hear a car engine, and footsteps running.
You will hear a gun. You will see the dream of my greatness in the
garden. It will let you pass."
She, in her black coat and hat, bends to retrieve his car keys.
When she looks up he has gone, and there is snow in her hand.
She is pale, her face arranged like the parts of a puzzle.
That she smiles at all
is a miracle.

Some evening the telephone rings.

The world is suddenly far away, no longer inside me.
That I am alive, has surprised me
To be ugly like this is to be invisible.

(The lies are not here.)

Star
Dum Coelum aspicio Solum despicio

Oh dungeon earth, what record have we scratched on your walls?

The great singing of the sun is unheard.
The stars are dark and full of danger.
They look down on us, taking photograph after photograph
of a blood-soaked landscape.

We creep like snails through the dust of glorious gifts.

Make me a clear stream to see myself:
I will die of fright,
                or find my way.

Mirror

An ice-pack of cold air slaps through the window,
heavy as the old women in the change room—

they have bodies to frighten children—used,
                              like floorcloths,
smelling of birth blood,

bruised, plummy, fruit cake rich, thighs—
        a commentary in themselves.

The 'girl' gets the hose out, sluices the tiles; and

small girls, bodies like clothespins or stretched gym shorts,
spy from eye corners.

Fluorescent light, heavy as foil, drops from the ceiling,
shows lipstick in lip lines, grey hair prickled up,
                                    like porcupines.
The mirror replays

girl after girl with a brush, wet straight hair,
relaxed into clothes from the stricture she swims in—

now, its my turn,
"I cannot stir, but as thou please to move me,
Nor can my heart return you love, until you love me."

Time
Tempus erit

You drive fast. I put my arm around you.
My daughter takes photographs from the back seat,
one blur after another leaking onto film.
Your free hand moves up and down the line of duct tape
on the blue vinyl, an inch from my thigh.

Great prince of darkness, hold thy needle hand;
your bones are knitting me a garment of earth
I am surfeit with long delay:
will I be dead before we get there
and your clothes, wet leaves?
The road clicks, my daughter sobs. Hold your peace.
The glass exceeds the hour.

Eleven Short Poems for Mercedes to Draw

i.
This is a face I would love without question.
It is like unseasonable snow,
     or a green bathrobe at the door
          at noon.

A dozen blue-crested quail fly from the edge of the forest:
a web of force lifts them like petals,
    or like snowflakes sifting through a wall of dense flesh.

The air they scale is glass.
Behind it is a room:
and the sound
    of a cry   kept back.

ii.
We lie in the grass and watch the dry burnt plain of the city.

I hear the clink of coins,
the racket of birds
in sockets.

I can smell the rocks, the ruins.

Moonlight shatters. I take your hand, its
    knuckles of crystal.

iii.
It is not time. Pain is a silver bowl of oranges
passed by the nuns through the grill *and*

here are your sisters, Teresa and Frances.
They toss oranges, play catch as they cry,
    Angela, Angela. Where are you?

I smell coffee, see the children
put down their satchels.

Don't be late. God is in the courtyards, the orange trees,
a spiral of approaching wind.

Angela—Run!

iv.
They give you pills
to stop the painting.
Here one goes freely
among thirsty stones.

Your life has no edges

but the long alleys of Sevilla, *penitentes* shuffling in chains,
trailing blood in the street like a bull scraping
wet nostrils in the sand of the arena....

You sit, immobile behind sunglasses,
pretend it's a film

v.
Monstrous faces emerge from cupboards,
hand in hand for a moment, with a candle,

against the tall house,
the overlooking windows.

vi.
Here is a dress. It is called space.
What a small thing is spirit:

a boy on ice
removing skates.

vii.
Behind you is a room,
a moon beneath ice.
sunken ships,
a scorch of oranges,
the dead unburied,
a seed of pain the nuns make into cakes.

viii.
I pull you to the surface,
scrape a film of stars from your breath,

listen to your heart dive through cool sheets,

the sound of accompanying oars,
nobody swimming.

ix.
I will keep the children,
the dog in pursuit of ducks,
the sky this evening,
the goat kicking the fence,

    and the smooth sea keeping some,
and giving some up.

x.
It is called time.
It finds me through every entrance.

The nightingale in the field
sings us to quiet.
We hold hands,

hear the world unclasp,
wild horses loosed on the sky's scrim.

xi.

A thousand times I have watched you
board a ship,
the shadow of a mast on the water,
the ship like a mouth.

Beyond walls,
the snip of snow,

the screams like the double crack
of a biscuit...

at the end of a hallway where no one is,
we kiss.

Insects flatten to the hiss of a lamp,
the dead come close, their mouths in an "O".

Voices shout,
moved quickly up and down roads.

Notes From the Dead

It is not what you think:
the blue door

is a series of doors:
there are no moments to count,
there is opening the door
and the fall.

It does not hurt
to remember hurt,
and there is time, and a desk,
and paper,

and a pen that unscrolls these lines for you.
But it is not time
as you measure time, by the sun.
There is no sun.

Your sadness
is the slow stir of a spoon in a jug,
the knife as it irons bread.

I send you this
so you will know
that I remember
what was mine.

✧

So many questions!
(You will get here, in time.)

You are right
about the mind and its storehouse:
its buildings, the small rooms, the window sills.

A single paperweight
recalls

an afternoon—
the piano no one played,
rain on the roses,
a dog chewing.

My hands reach for scissors
as if there were a drawer.

The pen is a crow
dipping its wing.

I write all day:
no colour flows from the nib.
The poem is a handspan of air.

The sea surrounds me.
My pen, a star, could shred the heavens.

I wait here for my friend.
I will know her by
the poems she spills onto the ground
like cracked eggs.

The embryo lives.

I give it letters like this,
one heartbeat,

a crumb from my pocket,
the last thing you said.

✧

You have something to tell me,
and I you!

I did not know
how little you listen,
how you eat
when I might say a word!

Do you hear a child's breath,
feel the skin of an onion;
does the sea still open and close
around you as you swim?

Your ears are porches,
your hands a swing,
your feet the envelopes of a lost
manuscript.

Walk with me,
let me fill you in.

✧

More detail!—

several buttons,
the treasures of an old man's brain—

childhood was best—

more restrained,
musical,
its colour like Chinese poetry.

Paint your hands: let me see them.

Letter To Janey
for my mother

Is everyone you love safe?
Is the door shut,
the closet locked,
the window latched against
fingers of wind?

Are they safe at a table buttering bread,
boiling a kettle,
sighing in the rocker, shoes off?

Are they safe
in their blankets,
mouths breathing,
eyes black as license plates?

Are there no dogging footsteps,
or strangers behind them with a stretched stocking,
no sad stories to make them think

you died

set aside like leftovers,
like a run-over
like a sweater, stitches spilled?

Are they safe?
Are you certain?

Then, Janey, come in.

Letter to Janey

      My singing teacher says that you have to catch the line: the song is already in progress and you ease on board with your voice. You never start the song yourself: its been traveling in your direction since the beginning of time. She doesn't talk about endings,

but I believe the song continues after you stop.
You slide off, everyone listening follows you,
and you stand there together a moment on the sidelines
watching the song as it passes from hearing.

You can think of it as a train,
or an animal running because that is what it is born to do.
That's how I think of you, Janey—you're moving quickly towards me and away—
for no particular reason.

You're simply there, in one moment,
a small dark girl in trousers and a red cotton shirt,
lifting your arms to greet me. "Come on!" you said. "Let's go see."
You said nothing could make you afraid.

I've put an ad in the paper and I hope I will find you.
But I know you might be dead..

Watch your dreams

      "Watch your dreams," he said,
suggesting that acupuncture might stir things up....
I love the feeling, after the pain,
of energy shifting in my body.
I have been ill—is it making me better?

...I see myself aged four,
sitting up in bed at night and making hills and valleys with my knees
and the bedclothes.

My hands are moving small beings made of light
through this make-believe landscape.

Dreams: Howard, the rare books librarian, is driving a bus;
I own many glass plates.
There are voices as I wake up,
once my own asking if Charles, who died a year ago,

242

was now doing 'administrative' work.
Does he still have time to write?
Do we write after death?
Do we get to finish what we start?

Will you be there, too, Janey, in your play-clothes,
standing on the hill a little above me
in the long brown grass?
Still unafraid?

More Dreams:

Susan and I are in Sylvia's bedroom.
We are there because Sylvia's husband, Robin, a poet and our friend,
has died.
Because of this, I am to wear a green dress.
We explain this to Sylvia as we sit on the bed on our coats.
They are spread out as if we meant to stay;
we nest on the wide skirts and sleeves of black wool,
and on top of our handbags.
Our shoes are kicked off, under the bed.
Sylvia goes to get the dress,
Susan rummages in a dresser drawer
and finds a beautiful green lace bra.
This is for me, too. I put it on.
Sylvia brings the dress and she and Susan have it almost done
up at the back
when I wake up.

It is a dress unlike any I have owned.
A dress my mother might have worn if she had gone to parties,
or been permitted to dance.

It is made of taffeta, with a mid-length skirt, lace bodice
and a neckline in ruches resting low on my shoulders.

I don't know if you liked dresses, Janey.
I never saw you in a dress.

✧

I dream of more poets.

P.K. and Patricia wear bright beautiful dresses
at an exhibition of my 'suspended' work.
These are poems that are also drawings,
and they are hung thus,

encased in Plexiglas.
Fingerprints on the surface show
where they have been touched.
At the reception P.K. eats only raspberries and asparagus
and has a special plate;

Patricia has brought two royal plates for herself:
they are decorated with Queens.
When they are mixed in with the other dishes
as the restaurateur clears up,
we insist that he find them.

Small gifts are provided for everyone.

There would have been something for you, Janey, if you had come.

✧

I dreamed this, Janey:

The house laid out in a flagged lane,
tall buildings round—
steel for light, stone for air.
The house is plain as shoes,
planked green.

On the kitchen stove is a timer
turned upright,
on the tablecloth—jam and spoon.

The calendar is dried to ribbons.

Stove out, ashes heaped,
a bucket of water holding
the form of water, its meniscus
firm;

a sitting room, two soft chairs,
floral curtains;
and there is coal in the grate,
slippers,
the soft soapscrub
of passages.

I touch the mantle shelf.
A woman watches from the walls
and smiles. Not myself.

Mixed in with the

Mixed in with the daisies are buttercups:
their long grassy stems tangle with the
sharp bitter leaves of the daisies.
These are weeds and they taste like weeds.
I've tasted all the flowers.
My fingers run up a stem to a transparent gob of cow spit.
I sit in the field and split a stem with my thumbnail.

I'm stooped over, looking down, at the base of a birch tree.
Behind me is the lake.
Blue and grey water lap at the muddy shore.
The water is dark grey and dark blue where there are fish.
I examine the exposed roots of the tree
and the red and orange leaves that lie over them.

The colours fill my eyes like fish in a bowl.

Colours are words: they fall from the mouth
of a brown-haired man wearing a brown suit.

Words are also gold coins, and they join, in clinks, into chains.
The jewelry of words scatters over the congregation.

Each word comes from the earth as do flowers and leaves
and the water that puddles the earth after rain.
Words fill my mother's jam jars on the table:
they are absolute, absolutely true.

✧

At my window, Janey, in my grandmother's house—:

Apple trees strung green and gold,
dead fruit and new together on the branches;

the coved corners, the window frame,
a shadowed floor of lights—
eyes pressed to colour by a fist.

They—the light ones—rub hands together,
touch me in the small knots at cheekbone
and ear hammer.
I believe what I am allowed.
Blow them out.

✧

In winter I trace lines of frost on the glass.
The white patterns are a netting of air.
There are ferns within the lace net,
and the fossil lines of lichen and shells.
Somewhere beyond the fields and barns outside the window,
back of the hill
and at the end of long roads is the white sea.

But listen: at night, in winter, the road is *gelid obsidian*.
I know these words because I know black smoothness,
the way it swells and subsides. The road. The darkness.
I know the right words when I find them.

When you put your hand in a cold sea at night, the sea changes.

There were no words to tell about you.

The man stands on a platform.
We are born so that we may die, he says.
And I see—
the me that holds an apple and eats it, making a wheel round
the middle, then eating the 'spokes' at each end—
this me is already dead.
After a while he kneels on the red platform carpet showing the
soles of his shoes.

I lie awake at night. I am here and I am dead,
just like you Janey when I last saw you.

I watch the light on the ceiling and listen for the sound of a
trumpet. When He comes I will be left behind.

I left you behind,
Janey, I ran.

I watch the door of my room.

I go into Sabey's garage and pull a chair under a beam
and take a rope and tie it round my neck.
I kick the chair away,
but the rope pulls down from the beam and slaps on the floor.

My brother comes in looking for me, his face twisting.
"You're supposed to be home," he says.

Somebody said this to Janey:

Earth to sun, planet to planet,
you are longed for—
as the body contains circle,

triangle, square, as the body contains
a vacuum.

Are you crossed pencils,
a compass of geometry,
the stars' fall into the oblivion of eye?

Or that broken twig between
the deer looking up
and a raven flying a trackway
of stones?

The wild is drawn in a circle,
the real beats through
the palm of my hand.

*She tells the story
to her imaginary friend, Kerry, in an accent*

When you are jist a baby they take you.
They wrap you up in a shawl that belonged to yr granny
and they take you to the church. It is such a big church,
with a balcony and a pipe organ
and pillars lik the ones they tied Samson to.
If you sits at a wall end you canna see round the pillars.

So I liks to sit next to the aisle, and I cn turn around and see the
mommies and daddys when they stand at the back until the preacher
notices them and he calls out:
Who brings this child?
And they answer, We do, and he says,
Bring the child forth. And the wee baby is carried up by the Mum,
but it is the Dad who hands it over when they're at the front
and the Preacher says, Do you dedicate this baby to Jesus?
The Dad hands you over and the preacher takes you in his big paws,
with the congregation lookin on, and that's that.

You don't belong to yrself any more, you're God's, or at least Jesus's
and he can do what he likes wi you.
The baby gets takin out then, and you don't see it
until it can walk itself into Sunday School.

Then you see it, all right, swinging its legs
and cuttin up paper with scissors and singin little songs.
"Zacheus was a wee little man". They look so nice, do the little ones,
when they squat down to show Zacheus being wee,
and they don't know they're wee themselves since Zacheus is wee-er.

Kerry doesn't come to church, so this is why
I hav to tell him everything.
He stays across the road in farmer McCalls field.

McCall had a daughter who died. He chases us away from the swing
that hangs from a tree at the edge of the field. We've all been chased.
Though once I fell and got left behind and Mr. McCall caught me.
"What are you doing here!"
"I jist want to swing on the swing," I said.
"Oh," he says and then he goes quiet. He looks at me. I'm small
and I've got dark blond hair my mum cuts when I don't want it cut.
She ties the top back with a ribbon.
I'm wearing my favrite red overalls and yellow sweater.
I can say this, though Kerry don't care what I wear.
I remember everything I've ever worn. Even the blue leggings.
If you don't have to wear them, don't.
They itch, and the zippers catch.
I don't mind the muff: I've got a nice white one for Sundays
and it hangs on a string so you can swing it
when you aren't keepin your hands warm.
Mr. McCall says, "You can play on the swing whenever you want,
I don't mind, but I don't want those boys in my field."
I just look at him.
He says, "What are you doing playing with them?
They set fire to my barn."
I get a shock when he says it. Fires is bad.
I run away then and I go back twice to swing on the swing,
but its no fun swinging by yrself.
I ask Kenny and Davey about it and Kenny says,
yeah, we did, so what?

249

He laughs and I don't like that laugh.
Kerry you don't like it either, do you?
Kerry hides when Kenny and Davey are around, but he's always there.

So they take the babies
and the babies don't get themselves back for a very long time.
It happens. I know it happens.
Because all the babies aren't in the church, are they?

There's a door they go through, mebe:
I've seen it at night when I'm talkin to Kerry and its dark
and you can hear the stars hissing in the sky
like somebody dropped them in a pail of cold water. *SSSSSSSS.*

The door is at the edges, sometimes one, sometimes the other.
I watch for it, but its hard to see.
I think its the door Kerry uses,
because I never quite see him come or go.

So Kerry, here I am in church and there's a baby that's jist been taken
and the mother's up to the nursery where she can look
through a glass wall and see the preacher preachin
and hear the amens over the loudspeaker.

Two sisters liks to speak n tongues and I liks to hear them.
One stands up, right in the middle of something,
like an announcement about the choir practice,
and starts in. *Sheila ma koolnana. yahnava Kaya. Christo christo ma shiava.*
She is so thin she makes a straight line from her hat to her shoes.
She wears her hair in a sausage curl at the ears,
with the bobbypins stikin out.
You can never see the bobby pins in my mother's hair,
and I know how to put them in so they don't fall out, you cross em.
But Shelly Cowpats, that's her name, doesn't know.
The bobbypins dangle down her neck as she shakes and says,
Ya-na-na mashalavah.
The other one is the brown one. She stands up
when Shelly blue sits down. They don't sit together,
so I'm sitting in my seat with my head down
but my eyes lookin between my fingers
tryin to figure where Sheila will pop up, and then she goes,

250

Yea, says the Lord, My people are hungry.
My people are thirsty, my people have wandered long in the desert.

The day of judgement is nigh. Weep for the night is coming.
One man is taken and the other left. Thus saith the Lord.

I sneak a peek at the back and up high to that nursery window.
The mother is standing and holding the baby.
She has one hand up, praisin the Lord,
and I'm wondering what the baby is thinking
because I know and Kerry knows
that the babies do think.

A light is showing

from the windows. "That is the grandmother's house.
You must reach it before night or the girl will die."
But if a light is showing isn't it night already?
Isn't it too late?

a waterfall of slowly melting ice,
a weeping willow of gold coins;
a building is being renovated, carpenters working,
open flooring, nothing yet closed in;
a river of lava, tiny figures in a boat,
crying, surrounded by flames;
a silver rope drops from the cliffs
and the figures begin to climb.

What do you think of that, Janey?

The Newspapers said:

...before the pert, dark-eyed (Janey?)
...was found dead

...lying on the floor
...the automatic beside her
...the bewildered little girl

...and Sing Sing Prison
...and recent workers' revolt
...men and money for the Reds
...placate with consumer goods

and seven year old Janey tumbled,
having gone there with her parents....

A Picture in a Book

On Sundays after church and a roast beef lunch,
we have to be quiet.
My grandparents nap upstairs and my parents downstairs
in their bedroom in the basement.
We are not allowed to look at comics,
and I am too young to read.
There is one book in the little bookcase in the living room,
with a picture in it. The book has a red cover.
I take it down and open to the illustration.

In the Coliseum are six levels of seating:
the lowest row is at the same height
as the top of the doors on a large gate that opens into the arena.

The perimeter of the arena is studded with crosses,
three to the left of the gate and six to the right.
A naked human is tied to each.
Five of these people have been set alight.
Tendrils of smoke rise from the feet of the martyr on the sixth cross.

A group of men, women and children kneel on the earth nearby.
A white-haired man stands gazing heavenwards,
his hands spread wide, his arms gesturing 'why?'
In the left foreground is a lion, his muscles tensed
as he pauses at the top of a ramp leading

from underground cells to the arena floor.
His tail sticks straight out from his haunches
and curls up at the end.

At his feet, and waiting to follow him, are a tiger and another lion.

I am not much interested in the spectators,
but I examine the martyrs for hints as to my own future,
although I cannot imagine the lion moving towards them.

He isn't looking there.
He is gazing upwards at a far away hill.

Looking for you, Janey

Across the fields

an old landscape—
long golden grass,
a single cow,
a wooden cottage next to a river,
the road a track between mud flats.

In summer there's a cow,
in fall ducks and geese: the winter
skaters knee and bend
in crisp edges.

Inside the house—
amber floor boards,
green painted shelves,
nothing thrown away—scrubbed tins
and plastic spoons, a sugar bowl
cracked along leaf lines.

She stands in the kitchen,
fingers touching spoons,
clothes on pegs, a garden sweater
with the elbows out,

an apron, its blue ties knotted, pinned at the side
(fence at the back, river weed streaming,
children come, and gone in.)

A robin foretells
the rim of its flight,
white saucer it spins for suet and seed,

the old pudding dish
where summer larvae breed.

Sometimes

Sometimes, when the service is long,
my mother lets me lie down on the pew and lay my head in her lap.
I never fall asleep.
I love the texture of her dresses,
and her Avon perfume,
and that she is still enough that I can be close to her.
When the service is very long I look through her handbag
and try on her gloves,
and watch her looking at her watch,
worrying about the roast cooking at home.

Sometimes
I lie on my side with a comforter over me.
I feel sunshine through the cover.
I let my mind drift.
It is like one of the small wooden boats my grandfather carves
and sets sailing in a water-bucket.
But as I loosen my hold on it,
a metal taste spreads through my mouth.
It travels to the roof of my mouth,
up inside my nose, pinching my nostrils,
and higher to where it widens and spreads behind my eyes.
I 'see' through this taste.
My thoughts are in pieces
trying to escape the pressure of this expanding pool of taste.

I suck my fingers
as I lie beneath the comforter
and pretend I'm not there.

The taste is blood, Janey.
It comes when I think of you.

Kerry is the leader of the Kenneth street gang.
Kenneth street runs along the west side of my grandparents' house.
I talk to Kerry in the darkness.
I know my brother listens.

Kerry is tall and thin and wild.
He is an orphan and can go wherever he wants to.
He lives, with the gang, in the woods and fields across the road.
He roams through the pastures of the farm.
He isn't afraid of the cows that loom large as buses
when I take the shortcut home from Sherry's house at twilight.
He doesn't think twice about the copper-head snakes
that are said to wind through the woody footpaths of Christmas Hill.

When the taste comes I don't see anything any more.
I can't see Kerry.
I can't even see the woods where he lives.
I am inside a white shiny light, light like plastic.
I hear the preacher tell me I am going to die,
that Jesus is coming back at any moment
that I am not ready.
I ask Him into my heart, as I am told to.
I say the words,
and I see the Cowpat sisters
and a man in a black coat, Mr. T.
He rises from the black water of winter coats,
pulling himself to his feet in the shadow of the bowl-shaped chandelier:
Yea, I have told you, the Lord is returning,
make ready for His coming,
He will come in the twinkling of an eye,
and the saints will rise and the wicked be cast out forever...
Repent for the trumpet sounds!

My mind skitters like metal spoons,
rattling the white plastic.
The words, the prayers, the unknown tongues
are a wind that cores me inside out,
like my grandmother cores an apple.
My insides are scooped out by metal blades.
I am so light inside my plastic that I scarcely exist at all.

My grandfather dances before the Lord,
is blessed by the Spirit.
He sees an angel in the apple tree outside the kitchen window.
But I am not like him.

◆

Did you know that you killed a girl? asks the voice in my dream.
Yes, I know.

But I know in the way I know a dream:
sideways, through water and rippled glass.

But soon I will remember you Janey,
I will remember what happened.

◆

Not a cat to be seen here
in the stone house
the house with a wing
a hole in its arm
a ghost in the hole.

Not a window-ledge for a cat,
not a mouse rustling wool;
but stone cold as flesh
and a dim red room.

Here waits the ghost
afraid to go outside
where the moon skates

a silver line on the fields;

where the hospital sweats
and children dream their pain
is a balloon of ice

bobbling on the wind
to the horizon.

No one returns, and so the ghost
remains;
the turmoil beneath the floors uncoils.
The ghost catches its breath.

Why are you here?
Why stay?
But it is not yet time
    time   time.

My grandmother holds me on her knee
and reads me stories from the *Missionary Bulletin*.
She teaches me to knit.
I thread needles for her using the 'threader',
the black paper silhouette of a beautiful woman
with a thin wire loop for a neck:
you push the loop into the needle's eye.

My grandmother sings hymns and recites poems
from her grade-four reader.
Grade four was her final year in school.
She peels buckets of apples that I've helped pick from the trees,
and makes applesauce and apple-pies.

My grandmother has waist-length grey hair
that she wraps into a bun and holds there with rippled hair pins.
She wears dark print dresses and heavy beige cotton stockings.
Her only jewelry is a wedding ring.
Because of her 'feet' she wears carpet slippers,
sometimes outdoors as well as inside.

When I am near her I am warm and calm and hopeful and alive.
I am free to think my thoughts.

I help her make the bed and sweep the carpet.
I bring in sticks of wood for the stove,
and fill the kettle,
and stir tomato soup in a pot for lunch.
I watch her put up fruit, and bake,

and wash her hair in the sink and rinse it with bluing.
She lets me brush her hair.

I never think of you, Janey, not even once.

People come to visit her:
Mrs. Choy from the farm down the road;
an old lady who uses an ear trumpet;
people who knock at the front door to sell 'Watkins'
and are invited in.
They drink tea.
They talk.
They go, but they always return.

But you, Janey, you never came back.

Here I am, Janey,
in the moments before we meet.
It is a Sunday, a picnic after church.
I am wearing a dress.

Mr. and Mrs. Burns have driven us here in their car.
Their car is dark blue.
Mr. Burns wears a hat.
Mrs. Burns' eyebrows are brown pencil marks.

It is hot. The adults sleep.
Where are we? Near a quarry,
on a hillside of long brown grass.

I walk away, keeping my parents in sight,
my mother lying back with her feet crossed,
my father next to her, his sleeves rolled up.

Back up the hill, on stony soil, is Janey,
she comes towards me.
Let's go further, she says.
And we do—and see—
at a hut, and caved in earth,

two men—
the tall dark one with a mustache,
the other shorter, solid.
I hang back,
but she's already met them—Hi!

The dark one takes Janey.
I should go find her.
But I wait. I wait for you Janey.
I am younger: you should come back for me.

Then I do go, Janey, I have to,
and I come to a hole in the ground—
a collapsed tunnel.
Around the rim is dry broken earth,
dead grass, pale sliced rock;

Go and help her, they say,
She's hurt.
I kneel to look, my knees hurt.
You are there, too far for me to reach,
so white in the shadows,
and your clothes are different;
some lie next to you.
Janey are you all right?
You don't answer, but your eyes open—brown eyes—
and look up.

Go and help her.
She will die if you don't (the men say.)
I catch some look between them, and I'm afraid.

So I run,
and they follow.
I run, and they are so close, Janey,
but my brother is there
and he says, "I've been looking for you.
We've got to go."

I don't tell, Janey. No one knows about you.

We drive back to the city
I'm in the back of the dark blue car.
I'm sick.
When I get home I go to bed
and I cry.
Is it a headache? asks my mother.

I wait for news of a dead girl.
I ask, at breakfast, one day,
if anybody has been found
in a hole
at the quarry
among the stones,
and my father says he knew somebody
who broke an arm that way
when he was a boy.

It is dangerous.
Stay away.

A girl died near Winnipeg in the summer or late summer of 1952.
Is this true Janey? I need to know.

✧

In the Archives of the Winnipeg Free Press, June, July, August 1952

a child who watched her father kill her mother with a knife
and then shoot himself;
a story of three small boys who were lost in the bush
but found and returned safely to their parents;
a fictionalized account of the Rosenberg case:
"I think I have a pretty good description of the atom bomb,"
said David Greenglass to Julius Rosenberg;
the "Dramatic Saga" of the ascent of Everest by Hilary and Tenzing;
a search, abandoned, for the body of a seven year old
who drowned in the Red River.

No Janey.

✧

I would know you

I would know you
anywhere,
if you were there,

but you slip through the mesh of memory
like a small silver fish.

I hear the pulse
of my navel,
my heart like a worm
dangled to the universe:

and they come, without you, Janey,
the silver ones, the gold, the very old,
their hands brush the pain through.

Please give me this,
what I cannot name,
what I desire and will die for—

not bone or song
or the journey from the cave,

but an angel who puts hands to the stars
and calls

bright souls
into my arms
as gifts:

a child who remembers,
a ribbon of time.

Janey, goodbye.

Gruta de las Maravillas

This is how I take my morning run, in the dark, on the
9th of October.

From the elevator at the ground floor, unlock the door,
walk down the marble steps and across the parking lot to the
small locked gate at the south end of the compound. I open
the gate and put the keys in my track suit pocket, say
good-morning to the two Guardia Civil in their bullet-proof
vests. They shift their machine guns slightly as they look at
me. I turn left and left again, walking through the red dust
in front of the bank to the corner at Borbolla. I look past
the Hotel Melia to see if Mercedes is coming. I wait a
minute, counting two orange city buses and six motos. When I
know she will not appear, I turn south and cross La Avenida
de Portugal to the north east corner of the Capitania General
and then down the road into the park. As I pass the sentry
box, I hear a hiss, and I look back to see that a man
in uniform has stepped out of the box, put down his gun and
is beckoning to me. *Senorita, Senorita. Ven!*

Past the tiled walls of the government building, past
the four dogs who sleep against its walls, past the tall
dusty palm trees and the doves just waking up in the
branches, then left once more down the broad park avenue.
There are small groups of men, dressed in orange coveralls,
pulling dustcarts spiked with brooms. They whistle as I run
through a pool of light. At the end of the avenue is the
coffee kiosk. The man who owns it, knows my footsteps. He
shifts away from his T.V.—I hear the quick scrape of the
rubber wheels on his chair. Come here, come here, he says.
Come and fuck me. Green wrought-iron chairs, wooden tables,
horse droppings from the horse-drawn carriages, the plaintive
bleating of the donkeys, housed in concrete bunkers, as they
sense the dawn. I am panting now, trying to slow my
breathing and lengthen my stride. A figure comes out of
the trees as I turn up the avenue through the centre of the
park. I feel a stab of fear, but he stays still as I pass. I
can smell the oranges, and then the thick rank odour of the
ducks and swans from the pond and island. A large silent dog
appears suddenly at my side. We run the length of the
avenue, past the lotus pond to the Becquer monument. Here I
stop for a moment to catch my breath.
The dog walks to the water cypress
and pisses against its trunk. There is no one near. There is the bust
of Becquer, taking off his cape, with two angels, and three
women, at his feet. I move deeper into the shadows and pull
down my pants, peeing into the dry earth. As I stand, I feel
a hand on the back of my neck. "Don't turn around," he says.
"Just listen. Look at the women. Love passes through them,
and around them. Either they are waiting for it, or they are
living it, or they remember it, or it is dying.

I meet the two other women in the park. Mercedes, the
artist, is large, with dark hair and pale skin. Her little
boy, Pablo, runs ahead. Blanca is slight and dark-skinned as
a gypsy. She is dressed in white. Her two children keep
quietly near her. We walk to the Plaza d'España. It is so
hot that the children want to swim in the canal. The smell
of dust and stale urine, of the horses pulling carriages, of

the donkeys towing cartloads of children round and round
across the bricks of the plaza, is all around us. It is the
smell of waste and time.

It begins to rain. Strange, twisted yellow
fish rise to the top of the canal's waters and gulp at the
drops. It rains so hard that the horses have to
turn their heads from the wind.
They are draped with huge black tarpaulins.
We shelter in a portico. When it stops raining, we rent two boats.
The children cry, and then they laugh as some
students rowing by, splash them. We come to a bridge.
Underneath it, boatloads of young men and girls mill and
crash into each other. We bump our way through, the boys and
girls aiming for each other, as if their only wish is to
kill each other and die. But they are laughing. They laugh
as they bump and tip, and as one boatload of boys begins to
sink. The boat fills with water, the boys leap up and
attempt to scrabble up the wall. In a moment the boat has
sunk and the boys are sitting on top of the canal wall, wet
and sheepish, with the girls cat-calling below. I row the
children back to the dock. We buy them lemonade from a
kiosk, and then we go home.

I sit on the terraza with my daughter, watching the other two women
walk away, their arms around each other.
They face each other and kiss.
They stop and talk to the soldiers with machine guns. I hear their
laughter float up. Then they turn a corner and are gone.

I can see over the building to the Prado de San
Sebastian. In the dust is a circle of ponies. They are tied
together. They go round and round for hours. They walk as
if they are sleeping, but there are great raw patches on
their skins where the saddles rub. You can touch their ears
and please them, but if you touch their faces, their bellies,
their flanks, they scream with pain.

Here is the house where we go to a party in April. It is
in the country. Parts of it were built in the 4th century,
other parts in the 14th and 19th centuries. There are
two Moorish towers, several courtyards, long hallways and staircases.
José Maria, who has a sharp pale face and swept back black hair,
takes me away from the others, who are eating long white
spears of asparagus and drinking wine, up to the library.
Here he shows me a 14th century book about dungeons. I
follow him down the corridor through the darkness, across a
large room under renovation, down a staircase into the
catacombs. "Down here," he tells me, "is where the Moors
kept their prisoners. You can see the rings for the chains."
I step forward. The space is narrow. I can feel his breath
on my cheek. "Over here," he says, "come and look into the
well where they met their deaths. Come, lean down and look,
I will hold you." He puts his arm around my waist. I lean
forward. His hand slips up to my breast. His hand does not
move, but I can feel the pulse of his palm. I look down
into the thin tunnel of the well where the Christians died.

We say nothing, scarcely move, hear nothing but the cool damp
air as it leaves our mouths, as it enters. We stay like this
while the sweat drips from us in huge drops, and with the
slightest of tremors—like air shivering through time.

We are lunching on the grass on a hillside of olive
groves. There is wild pine and roses, jacarandas in flower
which reach their multiplied arms in the air,
into the brittle copper-plated sun. A scent of rosemary and
flesh of magnolia stirs in the tyranny of the farm in the
valley below. There's a pergola, and in it are children
walking, swarming among the roses like fat bees, like
caterpillars, the kind you picked from my bare arms that
summer. We had a yard, not an orchard. You parked your car
in the shade and sat with me on the concrete steps. I lay on
your lap, turned my head, and took you into my mouth. Hot as
sand, granite, sand-stone, sea-splashed perfect. Then you

licked my mouth, my eyes, entered me. I can feel you
there now as I take the knife, cut the peach into quarters,
feed each one into the open mouths of my friends. I can feel
your hand as you tell me, Come, again, and you rock me, step
by step, into the grass, into the cool damp earth. I miss
you. I look into your eyes, into a smooth pool of
rain.

⟡

On the road to Araçena you tell me that you are leaving.
I am not surprised. We have been lying, side by side in the
darkness at night, without touch, for months. We have seen
the shadow of this moment, stretching before us every
day in the sun, growing shorter and shorter until now
as the car climbs its way through the low mountains and
the hillsides planted in oaks, cork trees, fruit trees and eucalyptus,
the shadow is on us. I smile at you and touch my finger to your mouth
as you drive. There is village after village, each with its
orchards and its wooden-beamed houses, rickety balconies
ablaze with flowers. On the eastern edge of Aracena we come
to the Gruta de las Maravillas. You buy me a ticket. You
come with me past the kiosks selling pottery and key chains,
into the modern wooden building where we wait. In here are
displays of stones of every kind. I read all the labels in
Spanish, English, and French. When it is time, you give me
the car keys, squeeze my hand and push me into the line. I
go forward, twisting round from time to time to catch a last
glimpse of you.

The crowd pushes through a tunnel and into an elevator.
I go down with them. When we exit we are in a cavern
glittering with light. I am numb with pain. I stand still
while the others elbow past me, then I walk slowly after them,
hearing the guide's voice echoing through the dozens of
chambers. White and pink stalactites and stalagmites. The
darkness and light of a film set. Nothing appears to be
real. Even the little bridge that crosses the lake could be
made of papier maché. I look down into the water. I feel
the rail give a little under my weight. Colourless fish,
colourless insects rise to the surface, then sink.

There is the general sound of weeping, of water
condensing and falling. There are swirls of icing, coloured
jellies, of earth and stone, light and dark. I turn around
and someone walks towards me so that we face each other in the
middle of the little stone bridge. There is no way to
escape. He puts his hand on the back of my neck
and pulls my mouth towards his.

I say nothing. I have my hands inside his tunic, his
shirt. He bites my lips, and then puts his mark on my
breast. He cups his hands under my thighs, and lifts.
"Tell me what you are thinking?" he asks,
I say, "Now. I am thinking of now."

Acknowledgements and Notes

The epigraph from Luis Cernuda appears in 'Words Before A Reading' from *Poesia y literatura I y II*, by Luis Cernuda. Copyright 1971 by St. Angel Maria Yanguas Cernuda, and published in translation by his permission. English translation copyright 1979 by Reginald Gibbons. Reprinted by permission. The entire excerpt reads, "Modern society, unlike societies that preceded it, has decided to do without the mysterious element that is inseparable from life. Unable to fathom it, modern society prefers to appear not to believe in its existence. But the poet cannot proceed in this way, and must depend in life on that zone of shadow and fog that floats around human bodies." My thanks to Don Domanski for drawing this to my attention.

My love and thanks to my editor Dave Godfrey, to Mercedes Carbonell and Ellen Godfrey; and in memory of Robin and Sylvia Skelton and Charles Lillard.

Anyone Can See I Love You
for Marilyn Imrie

I would like to acknowledge the contributions of Marilyn Imrie and BBC Radio Scotland, and the continuing support of Hetty Baynes. Several of the poems use words attributed to Marilyn Monroe in *Norma Jean*, by Fred Lawrence Guiles (McGraw-Hill, New York:1969), and in *Marilyn Monroe In Her Own Words*, by Roger Taylor (Delilah/Putnam, New York: 1983.) These poems were first published by the Porcupine's Quill, Inc in 1987.

Grandfather Was A Soldier
in memory of Edward Albert Grist

I am grateful to the Canada Council for funds enabling me to write these poems. I would also like to thank Public Archives Canada, Elizabeth Richie, Pierre Leduc and Brigadier F. H. Coutts. The work would also have been impossible without the support of P.K. Page, David Godfrey, Eli Mandel and foremost—the many hours of research, photography and encouragement given by Michael Elcock. In addition I wish to acknowledge BBC Radio Scotland, Patrick Rayner and David Dorwood. The poems were first published by Press Porcepic in 1987.

The First World War began for Canada when Britain entered the war against Germany on the 4th of August, 1914. It ended four years later with the Armistice of November 11, 1918. During these four years about 10,000 Canadians served in the navy and 24,000 in the air forces; 619,636 served with the army: this out of a total population of 7½ million people. Approximately 10 percent of all who enlisted were killed. Most of these were soldiers; as were those who were wounded—172,950 in the army alone.

In compiling notes to assist the reader with the historical context, I have drawn on the following sources:

Coombs, Rose E. B. *Before Endeavours Fade: A guide to the Battlefields of the First World War.* (Battle of Britain Prints International, London, 1979.)

Giles, John. *The Ypres Salient: Flanders Then and Now.* (Picardy, London, 1979.)

Goodspeed, D. G. *The Road Past Vimy: The Canadian Corps 1914-1918.* (Macmillan, Toronto, 1969.)

Hart, Liddell. *A history of the World War, 1914-1918.* (Pan Books, London, 1972.)

Nicholson, Colonel G. W. L. *Canadian Expeditionary Force 1914-1919.* (Canadian official history) Ottawa, 1947.

Sweetenham, Captain John A. *To Seize the Victory: The Canadian Corps in World War I.* (McGraw-Hill Ryerson, Toronto, 1965.)

Endnotes

1. There were no major battles (during this part of 1915) but the Canadians suffered 2,692 casualties from mid-September to the end of the year. *(Sweetenham)*

2. On April 3, 1916 the Canadian Corps moved into the Ypres Salient to hold the southeast part from St. Eloi to the Menin Rd., a front it was to hold until August. On June 2 the Battle of Mount Sorrel began with a German attack. The Canadians held a line that ran from Hill 60 on the right, included Mount Sorrel, Hill 61 and Hill 62, ran through Sanctuary Wood and across an open valley known as the Gap, to the village of Hooge on the left. By the afternoon the Germans had captured Mount Sorrel and Hills 61 and 62. The Canadian counterattack began on the 3rd and continued until the 13th when the old forward line was consolidated. Corps losses numbered 9,600. *(Sweetenham, Goodspeed)*

3. The St. Eloi craters were the result of gigantic mine explosions near the village of St. Eloi. The blowing of the mines changed the landscape completely so that in April 1916 when the Canadian troops fought there, confusion over which craters they held led to numerous casualties. Six British mines, totalling 73,000 pounds, were fired in March. Altogether more than thirty British and German mines were exploded in the area—the largest being 95,600 pounds on June 7, 1917. Two mines were 'lost'. One was triggered by lightning in 1952. The other still lies unexploded in an unknown location. *(Sweetenham, Coombs)*

4. The wholesale slaughter of the Somme offensive began July 1, 1916. British casualties for that day alone amounted to 57,470. In mid-August the Canadians left the Ypres Salient for training near St. Omer. By the end of the month they were in Albert in the neighbourhood of which the July offensive had started. On the 3rd of September they took over the front line just beyond the crest of Pozières Ridge from the 1st ANZAC (Australian and New Zealand Army Corps). The battle that began on 15 September is called Flers-Courcelette. The advance was to be pushed on the easterly slopes of the ridge on a ten mile front. The Canadian Corps was to take points of observation near Courcelette. An outer bastion of the Courcelette and Martinpuich defences was known as the Sugar

Factory. This was the first battle to see use of the tank. For two more months the Canadians attempted to take a defensive line beyond the Courcelette-Regina Trench. On the 8th of October most of the Corps was withdrawn from the Somme area to take over part of the Vimy front. The 4th Division (which had arrived in the Somme on Oct. 10) took Regina Trench on Nov. 11. The Canadians suffered almost 25,000 casualties at the Somme. *(Sweetenham)*

5. The Memorial to the Missing of the Somme is at Thiepval. On the panels of stone are recorded the names of 73, 412 men who died in 1916-1917 and who have no known graves. Behind the memorial is a cemetery where equal numbers of British and French unknown soldiers lie buried. *(Coombs)*

6. The Royal Newfoundland Regiment of the 29th British Division was decimated here on July 1, 1916. The area is now a park covering 80 acres. *(Coombs)*

7. The Canadian Corps spent the winter of 1916-17 in the relative quiet between Arras and Lens. Before them loomed Vimy Ridge. The ridge commanded the valley of the Scarpe River and the Douai plain. The Germans had held it since 1914. Already more than 200,000 men had fallen on these slopes. An elaborate system of tunnels to house concentrations of troops was begun as early as 1915. By 1917 there were more than 22 miles of subways on 4 levels. Farbus Wood is at the right (southeast) end of the ridge. The Canadian attack began on Easter Monday April 9, 1917. By the next day most of the ridge was in Canadian hands. (The Germans also had a maze of trenches, dugouts, connecting tunnels and concrete strongpoints.) On April 28 the Canadian 1st Division attacked to clear the Arleux Loop—an enemy salient in front of the village of Arleux-en-Gohelle. *(Sweetenham, Coombs)*

8. Notre Dame de Lorette is the French National Memorial and Cemetery. Apart from 20,000 in individual graves, another 20-30,000 unknown lie in the Ossuary. The ridge on which it stands faces Vimy Ridge. *(Coombs)*

9. In May, June, July 1917 the Canadian Corps undertook numerous attacks in the Vimy-Lens area (including Fresnoy village and La Coulotte). There were raids on the Souchez-Arras sector. On the

10th of July the Corps relieved the British opposite Lens and Hill 70. On the 15th of August they attacked Hill 70 successfully but had to resist 21 counterattacks. On the 18th the battle was ended. Currie (the Corps Commander) called it the hardest in which the Corps had fought. Hill 70, although nearly indistinguishable from the flat land which surrounds it, did provide an advantageous view of Lens. *(Sweetenham, Goodspeed)*

10. In mid-October 1917 the Corps returned to Ypres. On the 18th they took over from 2nd ANZAC in the lines. The battlefield (fighting had been going on since July 3) was a porridge of mud. The Canadians attacked at dawn on Oct. 26. It was November 15 before General Haig finally called a halt to the battle for which few could find justification. The Canadians, with losses of 15,654, succeeded in capturing the village of Passchendaele on Nov. 6. In mid-November they returned to the Vimy-Lens front. In the spring some of the soldiers began to farm behind the lines in an attempt to restore purpose and sanity. By mid-April 1918 the Corps held 16 miles of the Lens-Vimy Ridge front. *(Sweetenham, Goodspeed, Giles)*

11. Hill 60, in the Ypres Salient, changed hands several times during the War. The Germans took it in 1914, the British in 1915. The Germans took and held it until 1918 when it was retaken by the British under the King of the Belgians. The hill was blown to bits by mines. It has been left as it was at the end of the War as a memorial to the many who fought there and to the sappers who were in its interior when the mines were blown. *(Coombs, Goodspeed, Sweetenham)*.

12. On the 21st of March 1918, attempting to finish the war before the arrival of fresh American troops, the Germans launched a major attack on the Somme. By the 30th they had advanced to the fringes of Amiens. On April 9 they attacked in Flanders.

The British gains of 1917, incuding Passchendaele, were swept away in a single day, although Ypres still held out. By May the Germans were nearing Paris, and attacks and counterattacks continued throughout the summer in Champagne and across the Marne. On August 8 the British and French launched an attack in the Amiens area. The front was about 14 miles long with the French army holding the south portion below the Amiens-Roye road. The

Canadians were adjacent—north—of the French and the River Luce cut across their line of attack. On that day the Canadian Corps advanced their portion of the by 8 miles. To many, this was the decisive battle of the War. *(Sweeteham)*

Calling All the World
for Solon

My thanks to Don Mowat and CBC Radio. This work was first published by Press Porcepic in 1989. The Captain Dart quotation on page 106 can be found in *Space History* by Tony Osman (St. Martin's Press: New York, 1983.)

The dream of space, of travelling in space, has fascinated human beings for hundreds, probably thousands, of years. In the late 1950's, with the launching of the first man-made satellite, the dream suddenly drew within reach. Sputnik I was launched into orbit around the earth on October 4, 1957. This event, in the midst of the cold war between the Soviet Union and its allies, and the Americans and theirs, inspired not just admiration, but terror. If the Soviets had this level of powerful rocketry (enough to launch the satellite) the reasoning went, then surely their ability to attack Western targets with propelled and guided long-range ballistic missiles had been seriously underestimated. I remember standing outside late at night with my parents to watch the satellite cross the sky, with just this mixture of fearful wonder.

The world's second artificial satellite, Sputnik II, was launched on November 3rd 1957. This time there was a living creature, a dog—Laika—on board; and this time the world watched with different feelings. Laika was an emissary, Laika carried humanity's complex dream of discovery and adventure, of hope for something better and freedom from the burden of destructive human civilization with her. At the very least, we wanted Laika to make her journey into the unknown, and return.

We know now that a number of the early space voyagers, animal and human, died—the whole story has yet to be told. Perhaps it wasn't the right way to pursue the dream—certainly the fear of being left behind in the arms race subverted the more innocent passion for discovery and knowledge. But when Laika travelled in space the passion and innocence were there in full force; and so was the dream. It was this part of the dream—the courage and desire to link what is 'out there' with who and what we are—that I wanted to recall.

Love As It Is
for Stan, who sat me down with Chopin's letters,
and in memory of Margaret Wilson

"George Sand's Letter," which was first published in *Exile* Magazine, received the National Magazine Award for Poetry, silver. My thanks to Don Mowat and CBC Radio, and to the Canada Council, for their support. Excerpts from George Sand and Fryderyk Chopin's letters are taken, in the main, from *Selected Correspondence of Fryderyk Chopin*, translated and edited by Arthur Hedley (William Heinemann Ltd., Great Britain, 1962.) "Letter from Portugal" is a Glossa and "Madrigal, a Lullaby for Xan" is an English Madrigal. "Love As It Is" was first published by Beach Holme Publishers in 1993.

Autobiography
for P.K. Page

"How Were the People Made?" was a winner of the *Malahat Review* Long Poem Prize, and was published in Issue #108. Several of the poems in "Mirror Gazing" and the poem, "Interior Castle", were printed in a pamphlet, *Interior Castle*, published by the Hawthorne Press. "I would have wept" is a Rondeau. Lines quoted from St. John of the Cross can be found in *St. John of the Cross, Poems* (Penguin, 1960). The poems were translated by Roy Campbell. The lines quoted from P.K Page can be found in the poem, "The End", in *Hologram* (Brick Books, 1994). Quotations from Hamish Henderson have been taken from *Elegies For the Dead in Cyrneaica* (EUSPB, Edinburgh, 1977.) My love and thanks to Neil Solomon, Susan Musgrave, Robin Skelton and Michael and Xan Elcock. I wish also to thank the Province of British Columbia, Cultural Services Branch for its support. "Autobiography" was published in 1996 by Beach Holme Publishers.

When I am Dead and My Heart is Weighed

The poems in "Emblems" were inspired by an early 18th century text, *Emblems*, by (I believe) Edward Ben Lowes. "Letter to Janey" would not have been written without the encouragement of Don Domanski and Mary Meidell. My thanks to them both. "Gruta de las Maravillas" was published in *The Canadian Forum*, Volume LXXV, Number 856, January/February 1997.